Are Bones Bendy? Biology for Kids
Children's Biology Books

BABY PROFESSOR

EDUCATION KIDS

Speedy Publishing LLC
40 E. Main St. #1156
Newark, DE 19711
www.speedypublishing.com
Copyright 2016

How strong are your bones? Can
you bend them?
Are the bones in your
skeleton flexible?

Let's talk about the human skeleton. Do you have an idea of how amazing your skeletal system is?

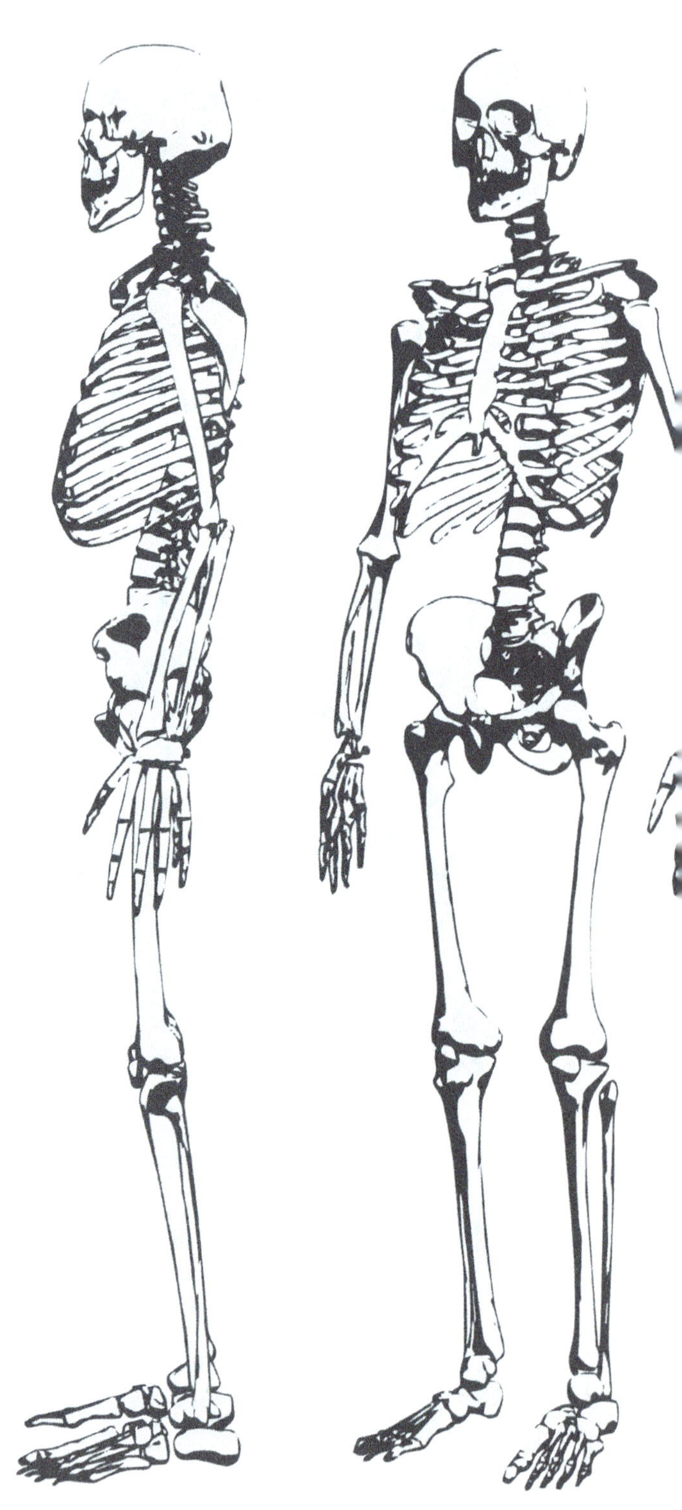

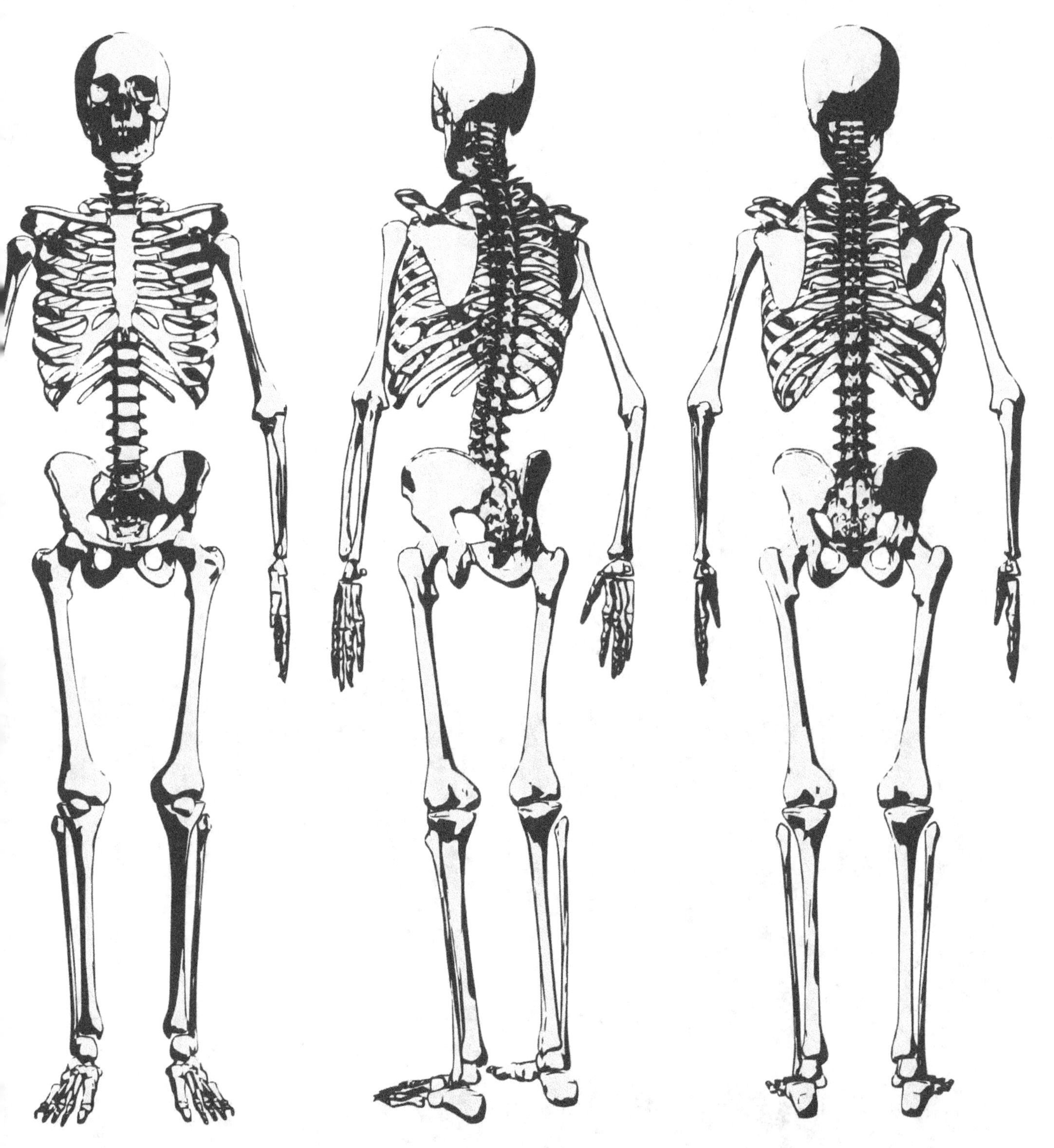

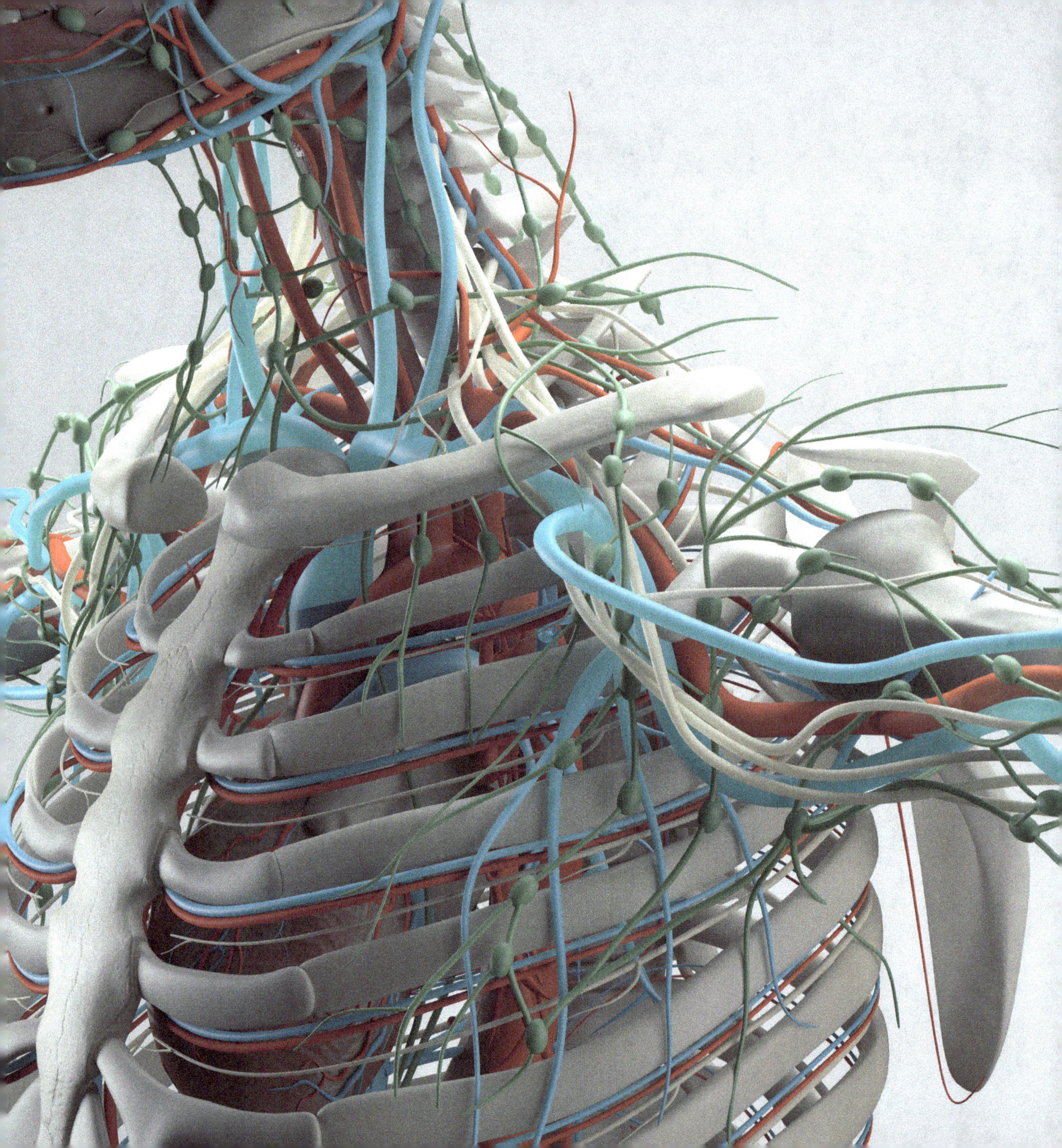

Our skeletal system performs many important functions. It supports the body for movement.

It is in charge of the production of blood cells. The skeletal system also protects our inner organs.

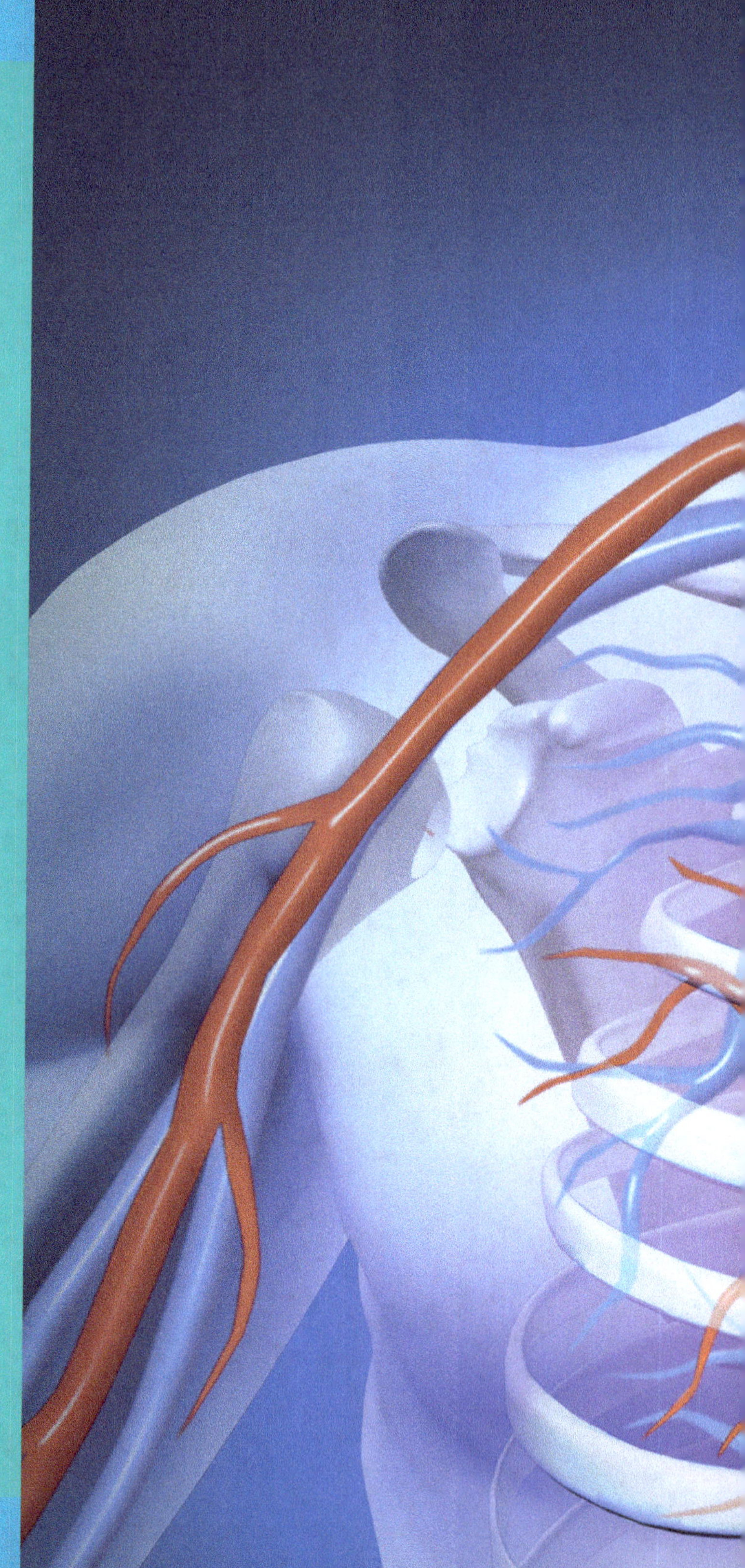

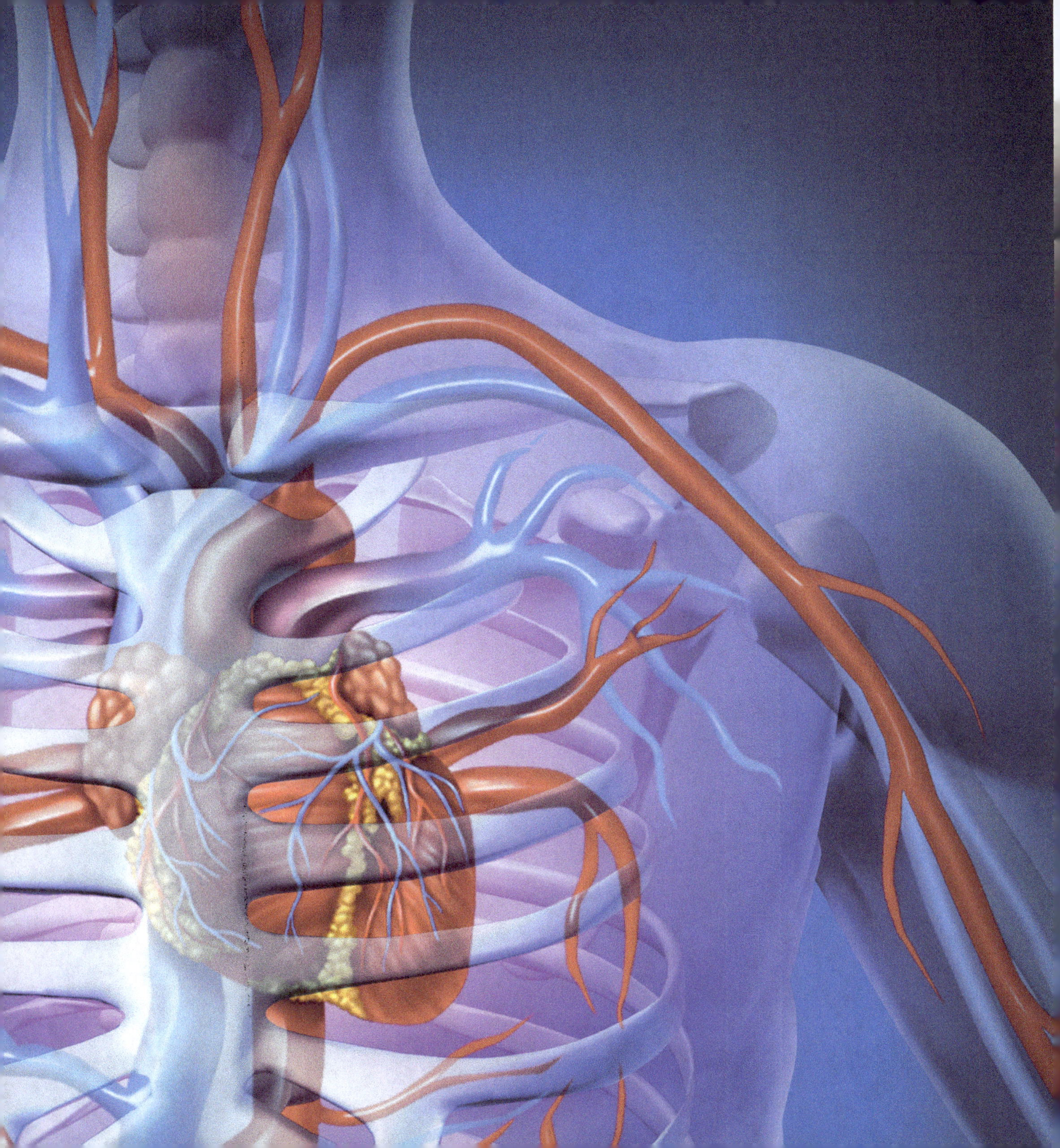

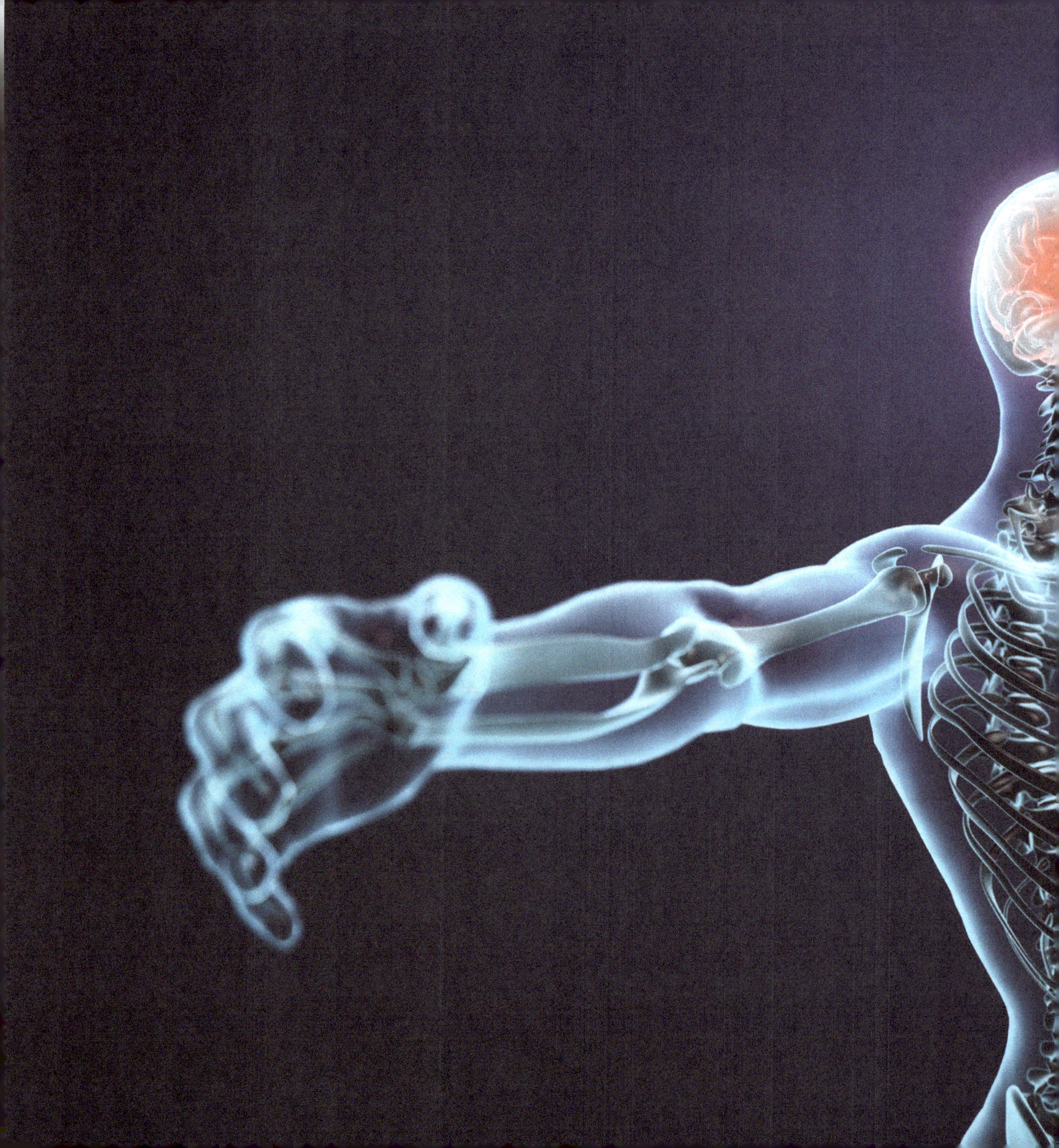

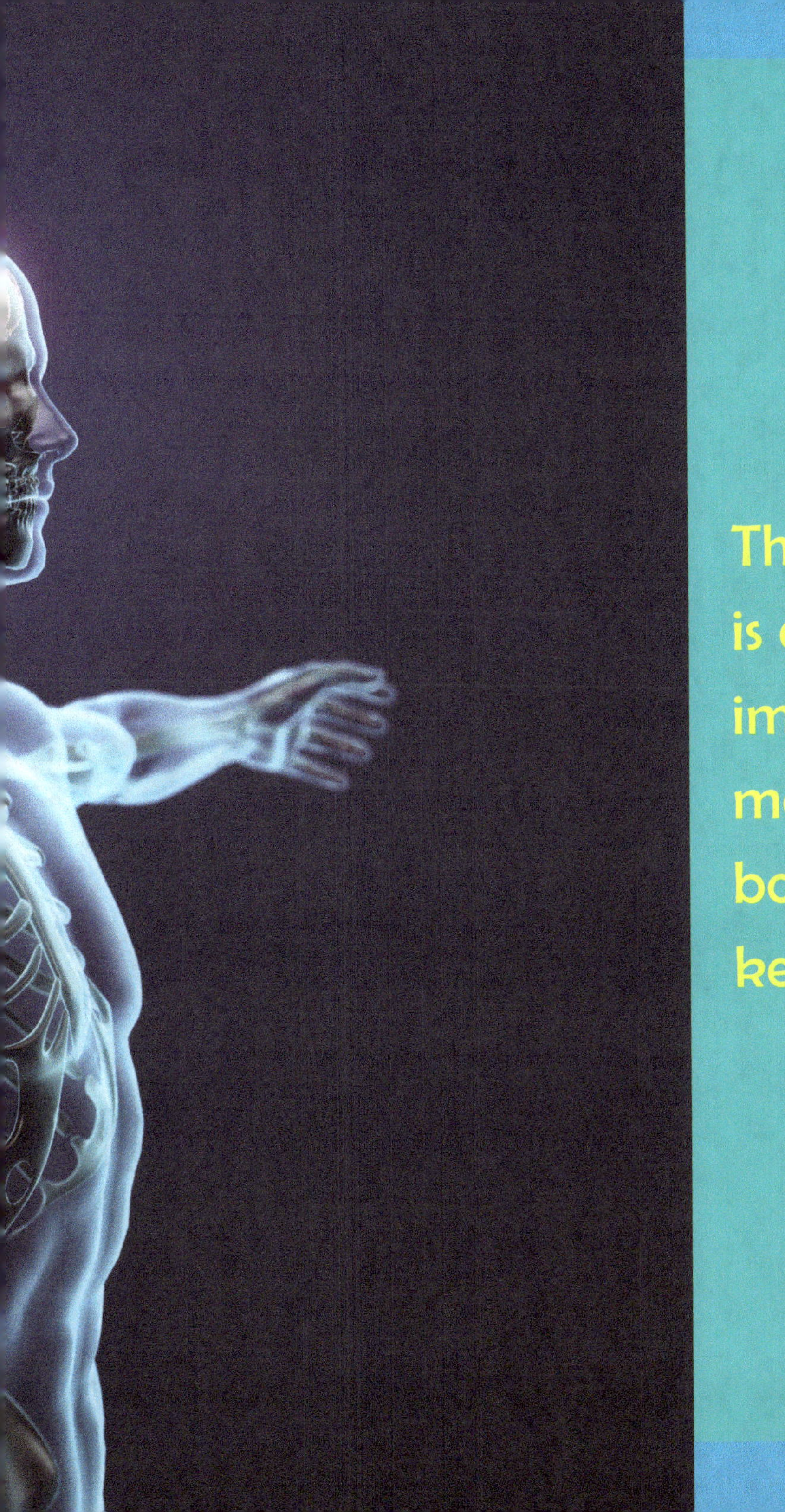

That is why it is extremely important to maintain our strong bones. We have to keep them healthy.

Have you noticed
your mother telling
you to always drink
your milk?

Milk has calcium.
Our bones need
calcium to be strong
and healthy.

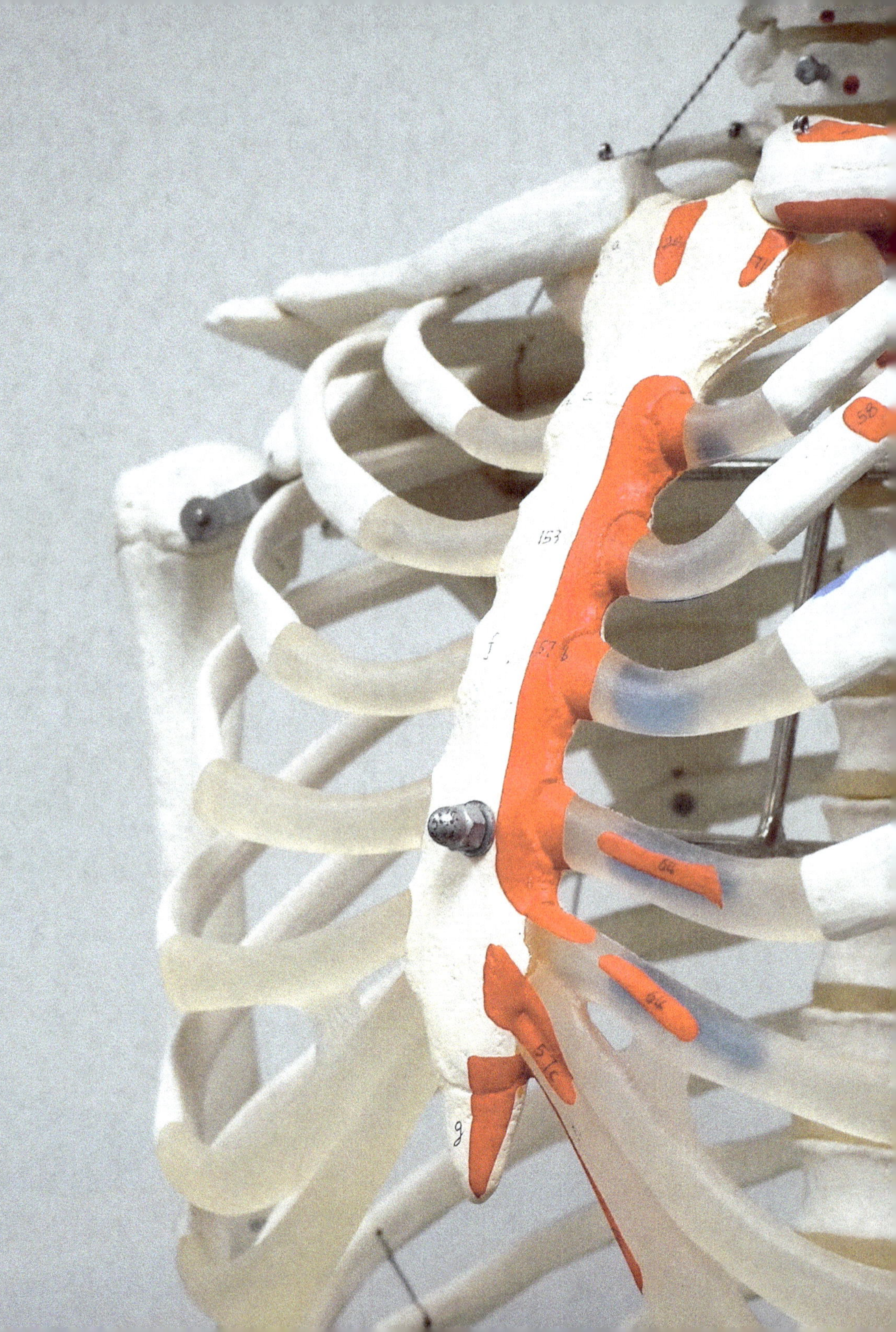

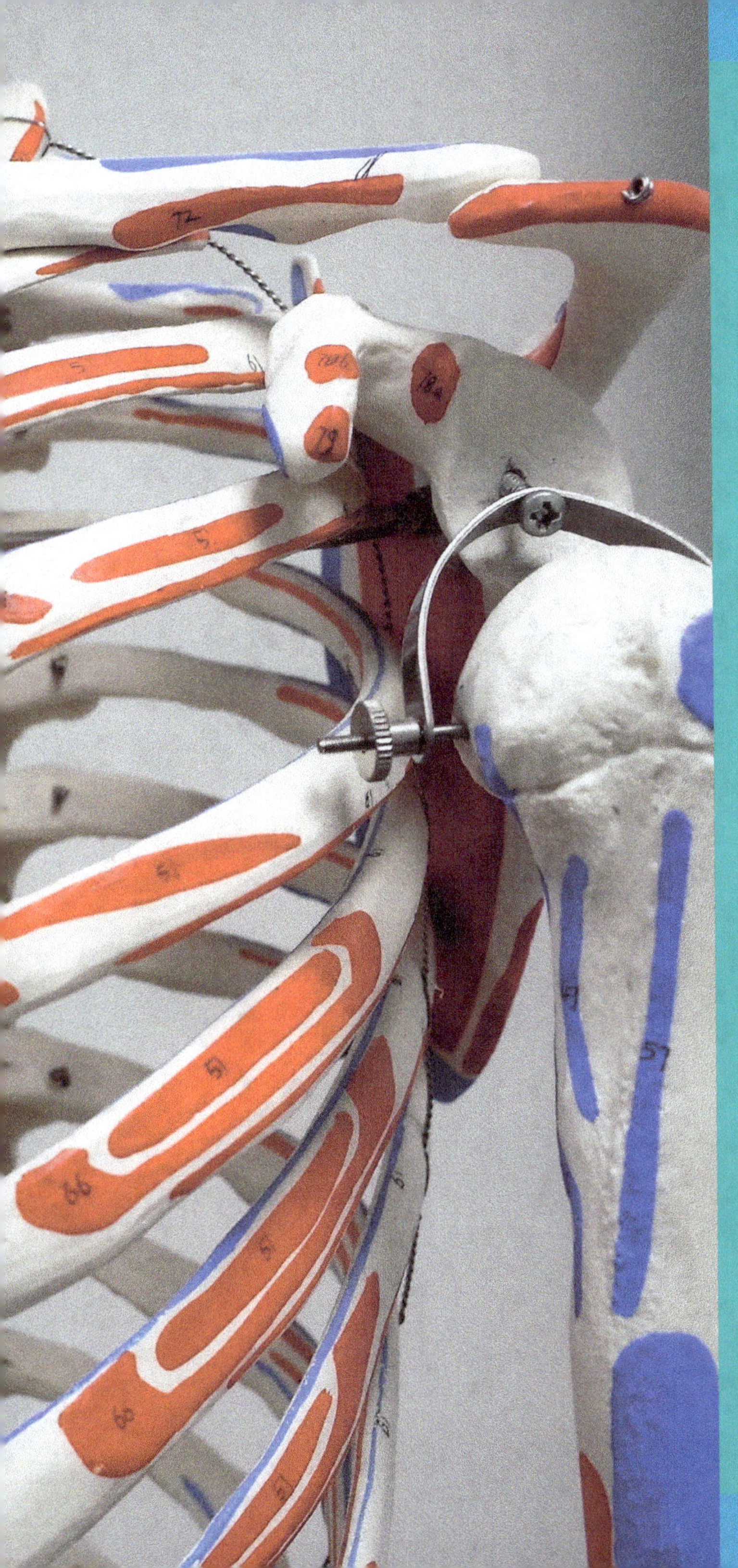

Around 300 bones make up the human skeleton at birth. As the person grows to adulthood, some of the bones join and fuse together and give us a total of 206 bones.

The inner
framework of
our bones is the
skeleton. Our
bones give shape
to our body.

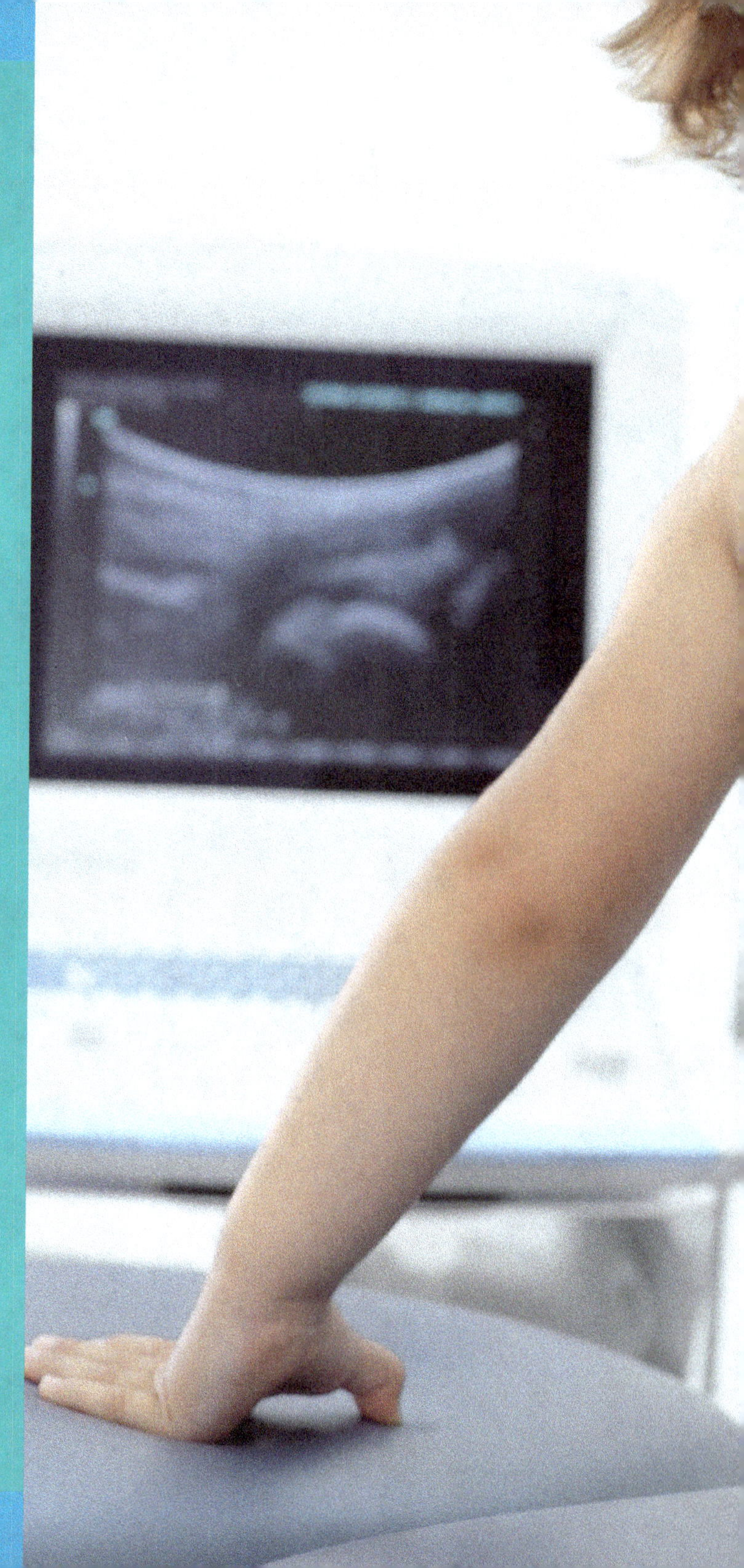

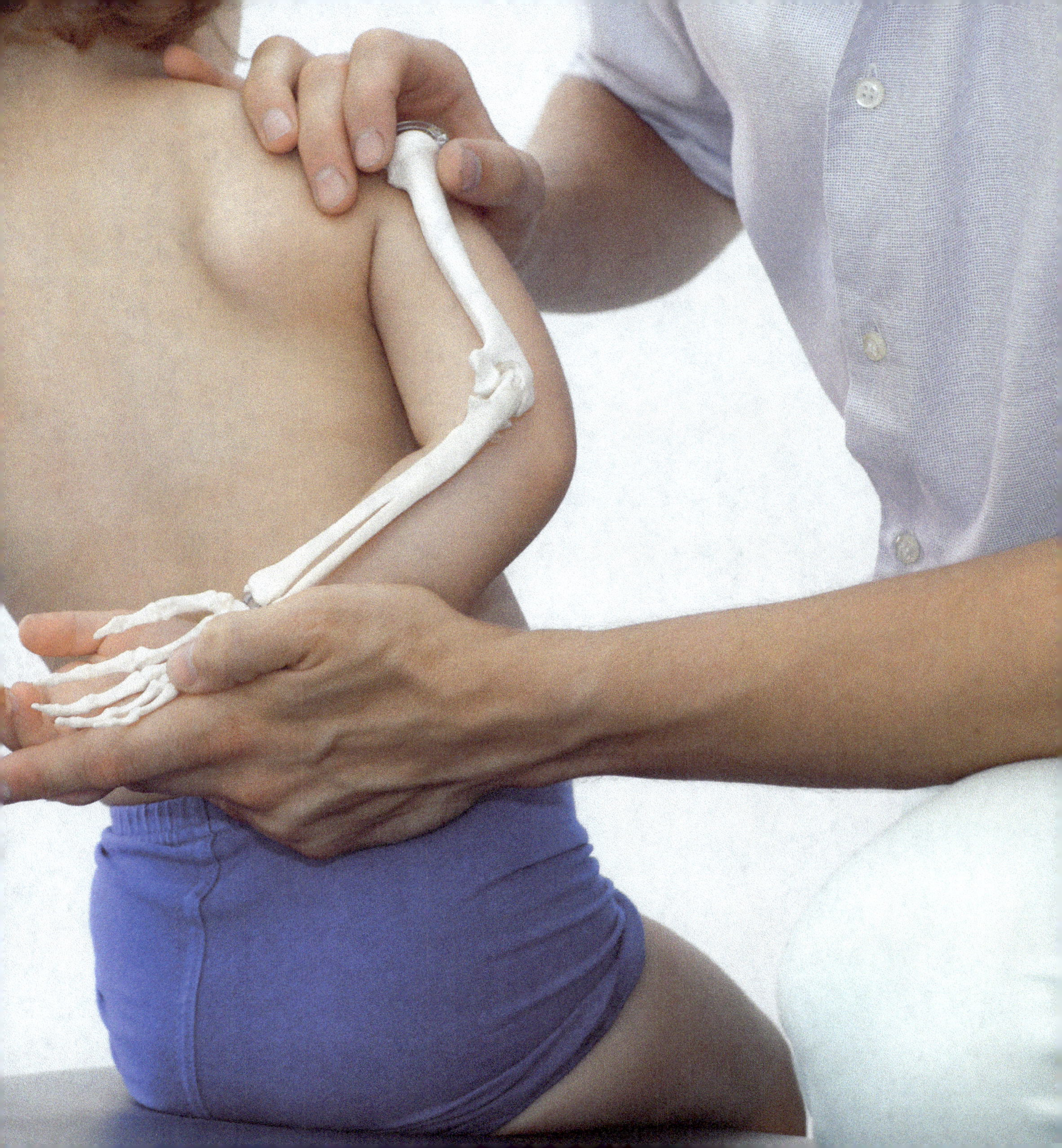

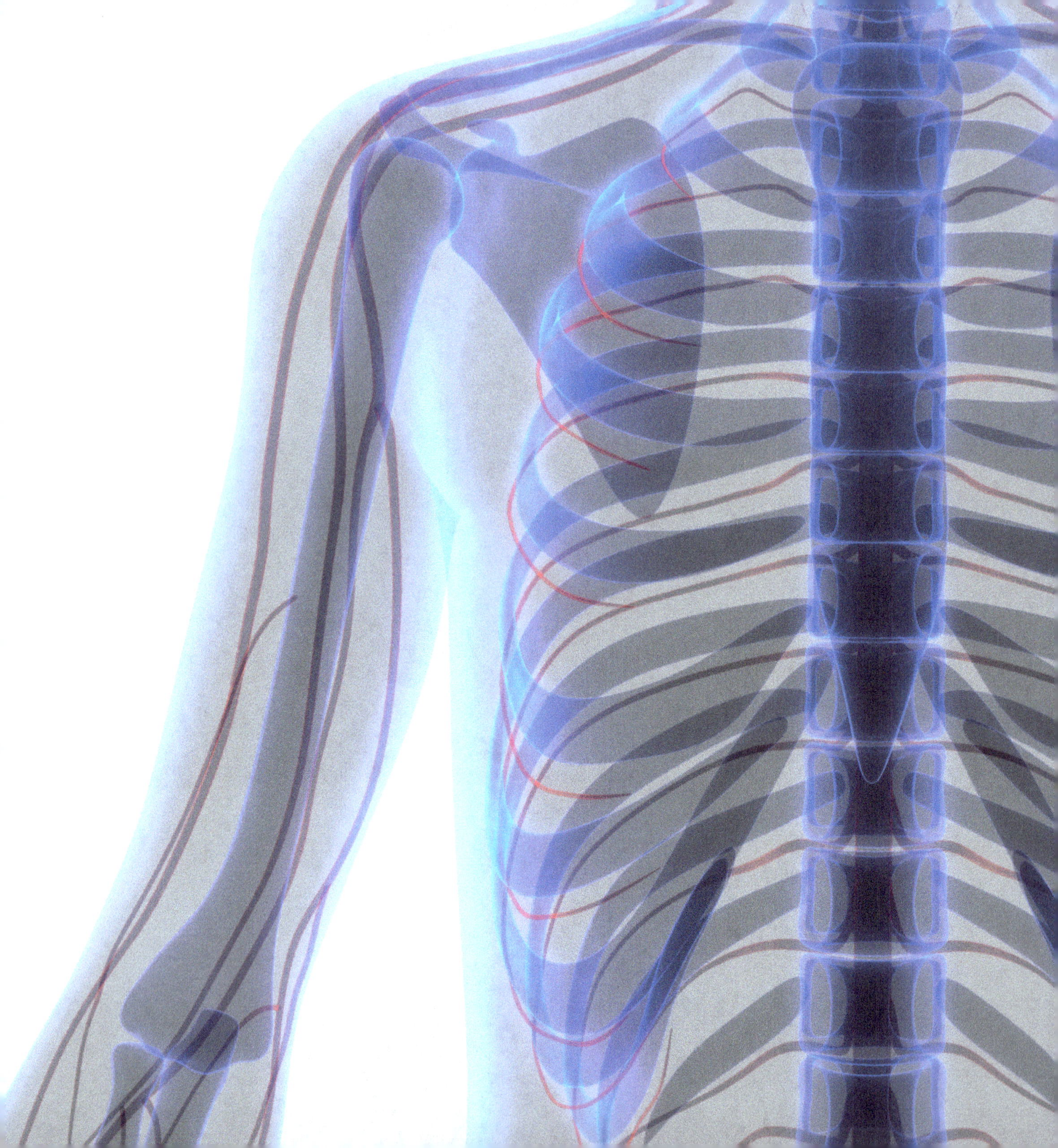

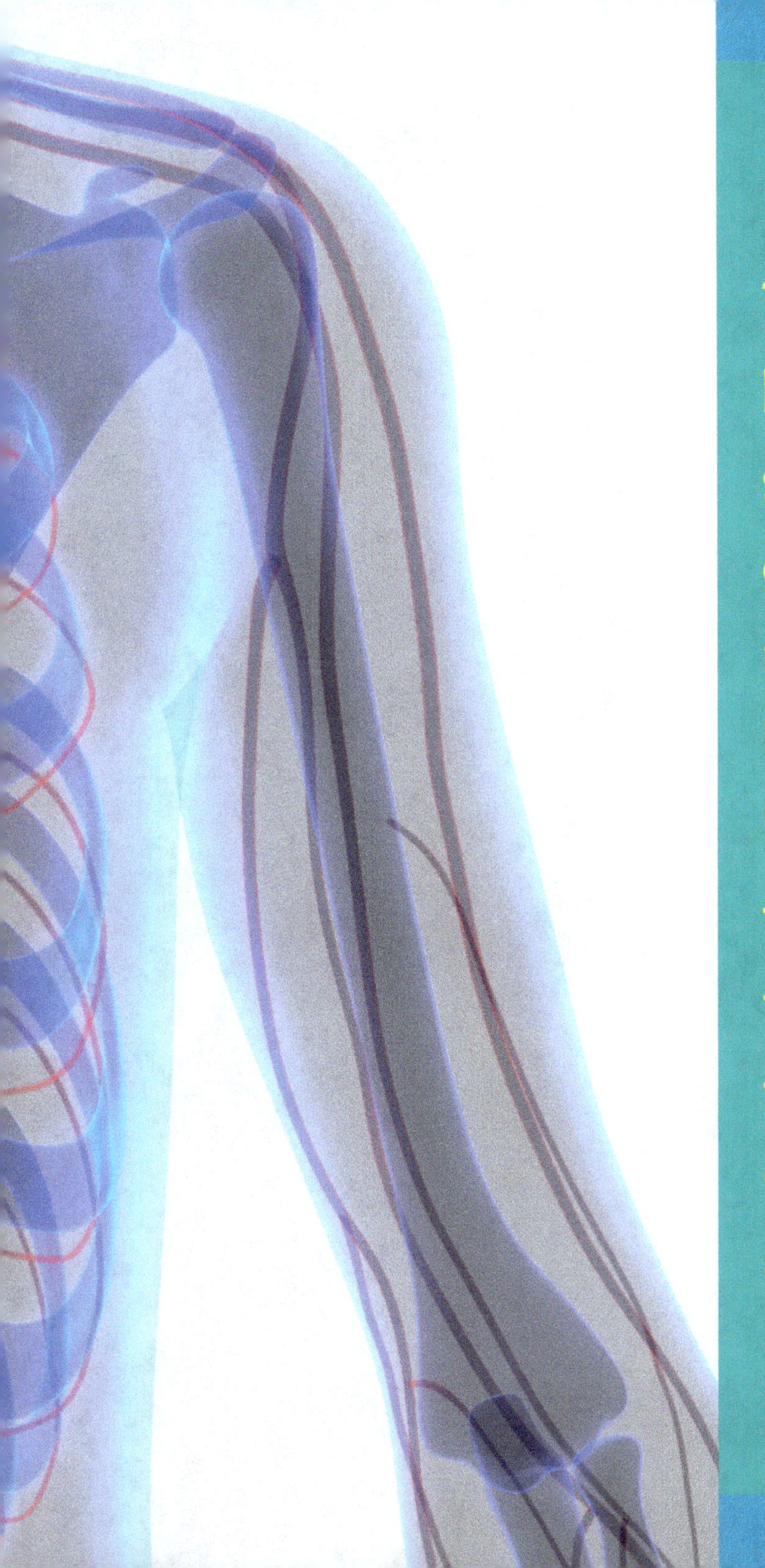

They support our body so we can stand upright and to make movements. The largest and the longest among the bones is the thighbone, or the femur, while the smallest are the ossicle bones.

These tiny bones
are also known as
staples or stirrups.
They are found
in the inner ear.

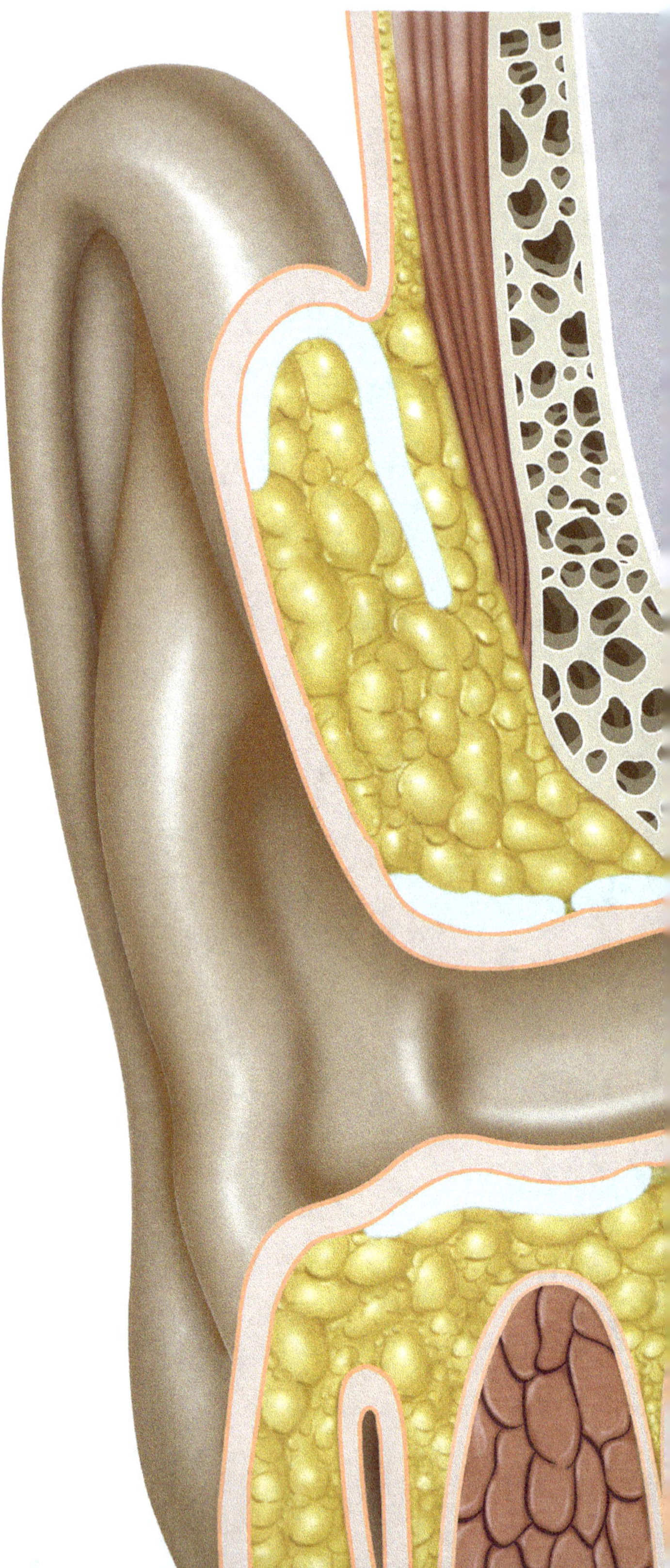

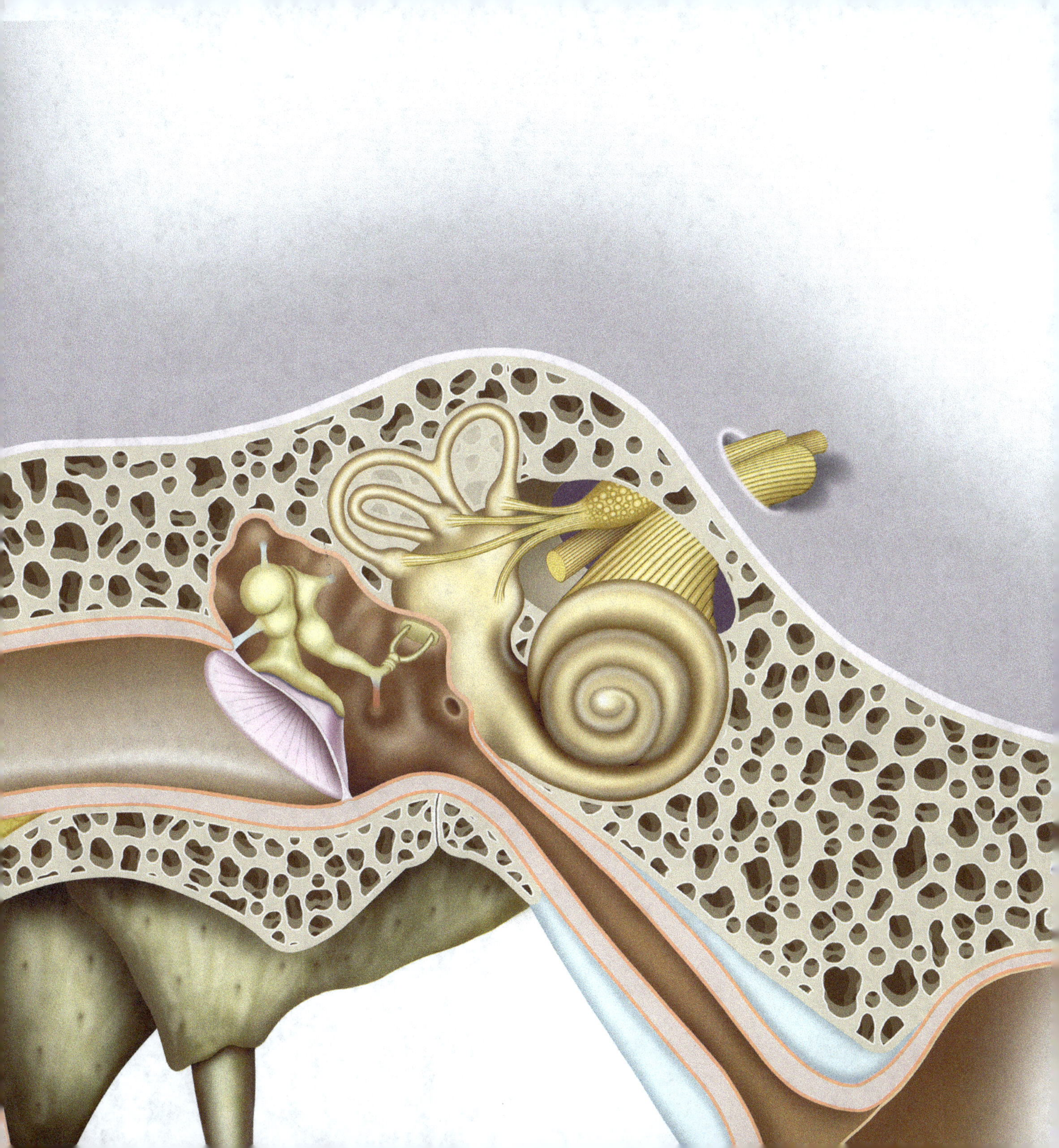

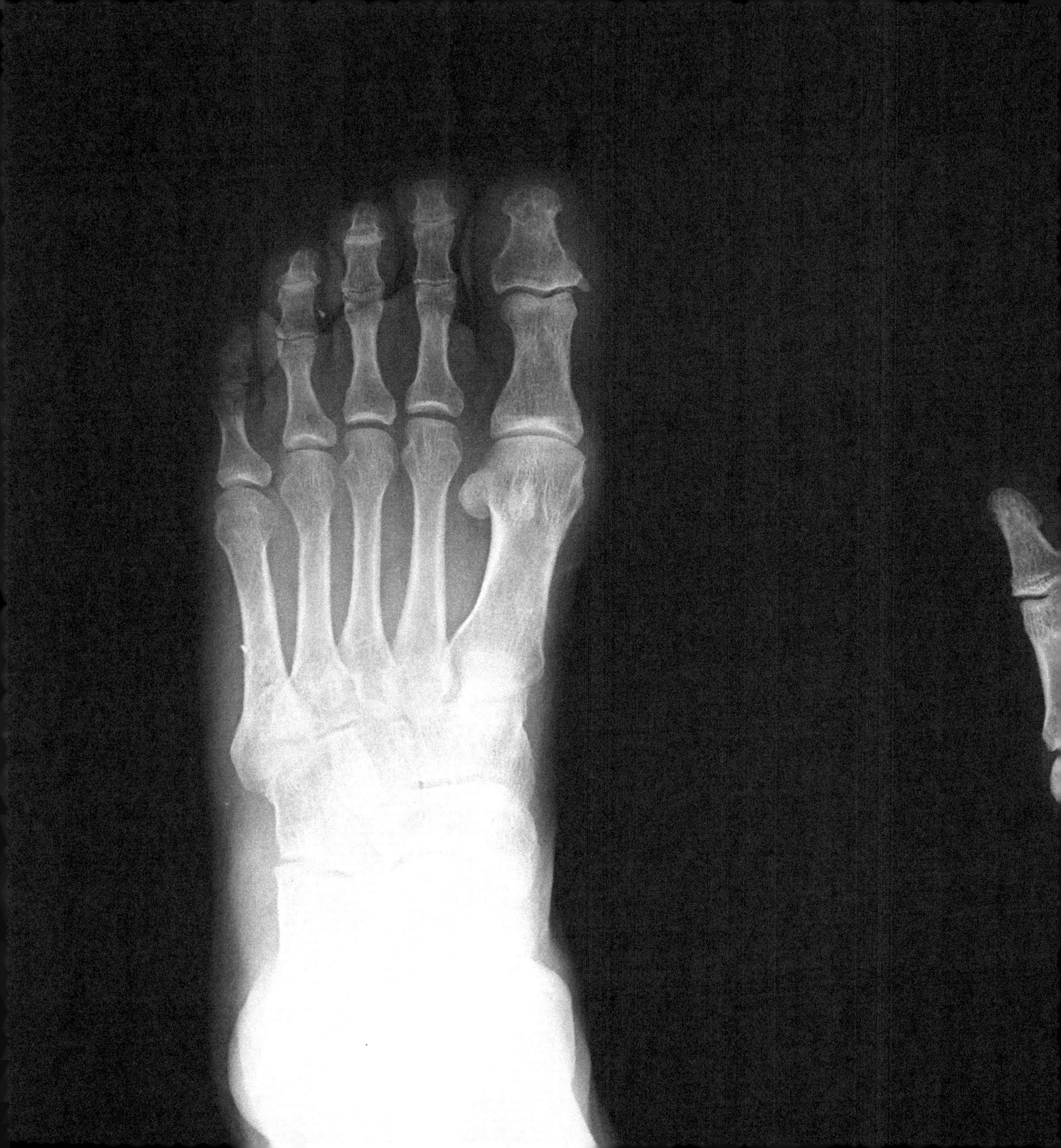

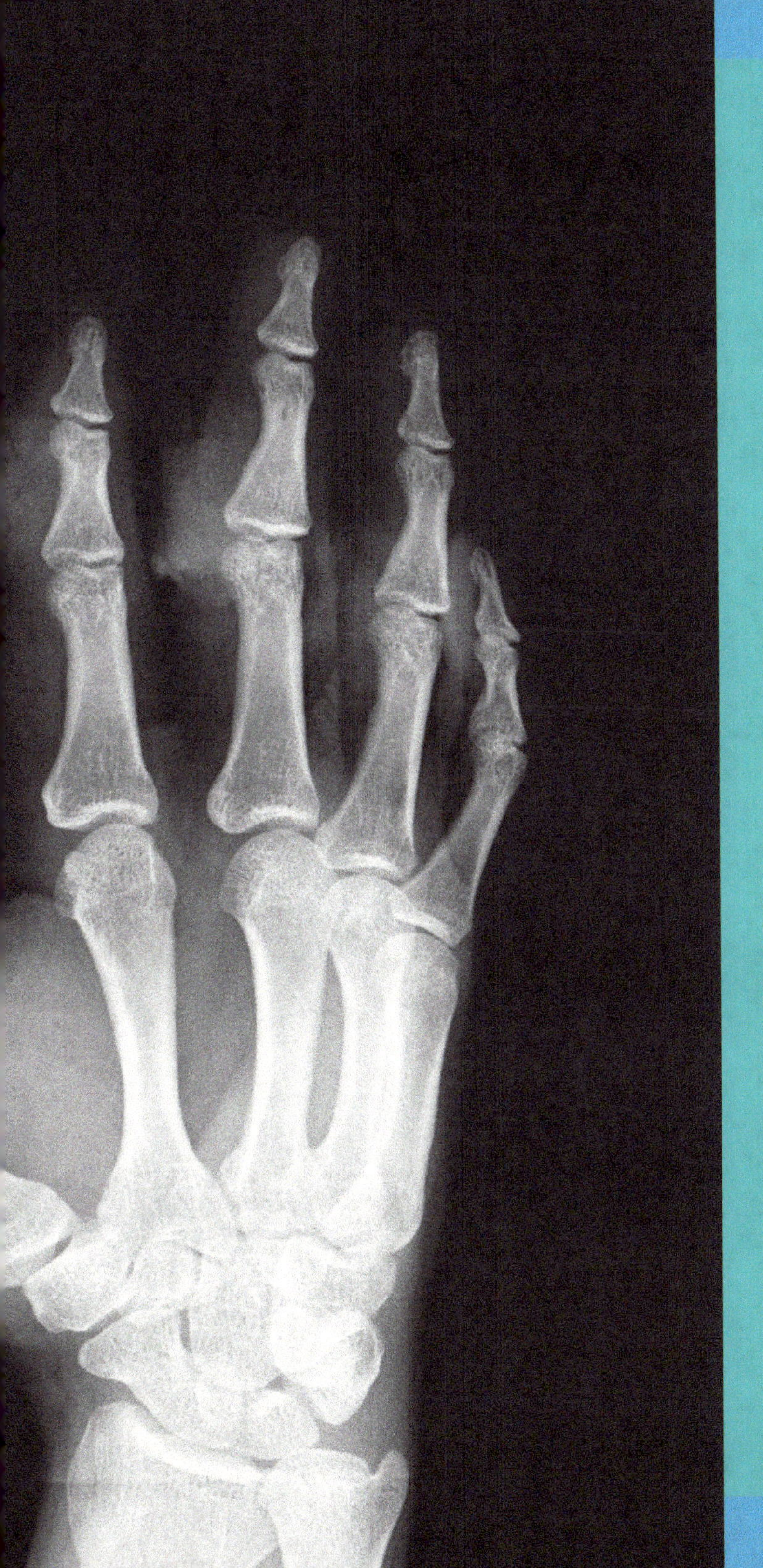

The bones in the hands and feet of an adult make up more than half of the bones in the body.

Our bones are very
strong. They can
be compared to
steel. In fact, bones
are considered
five times stronger
than steel.

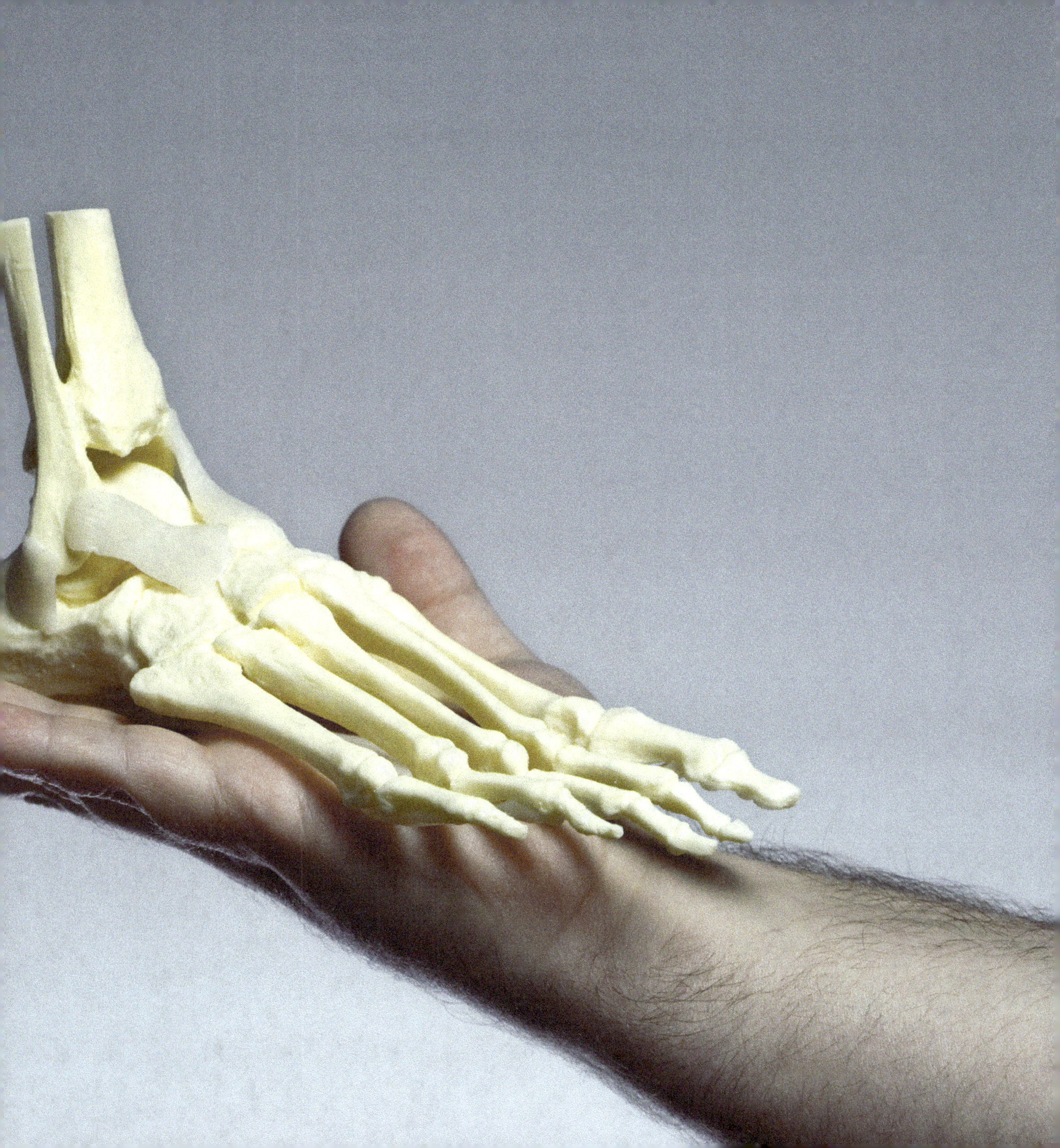

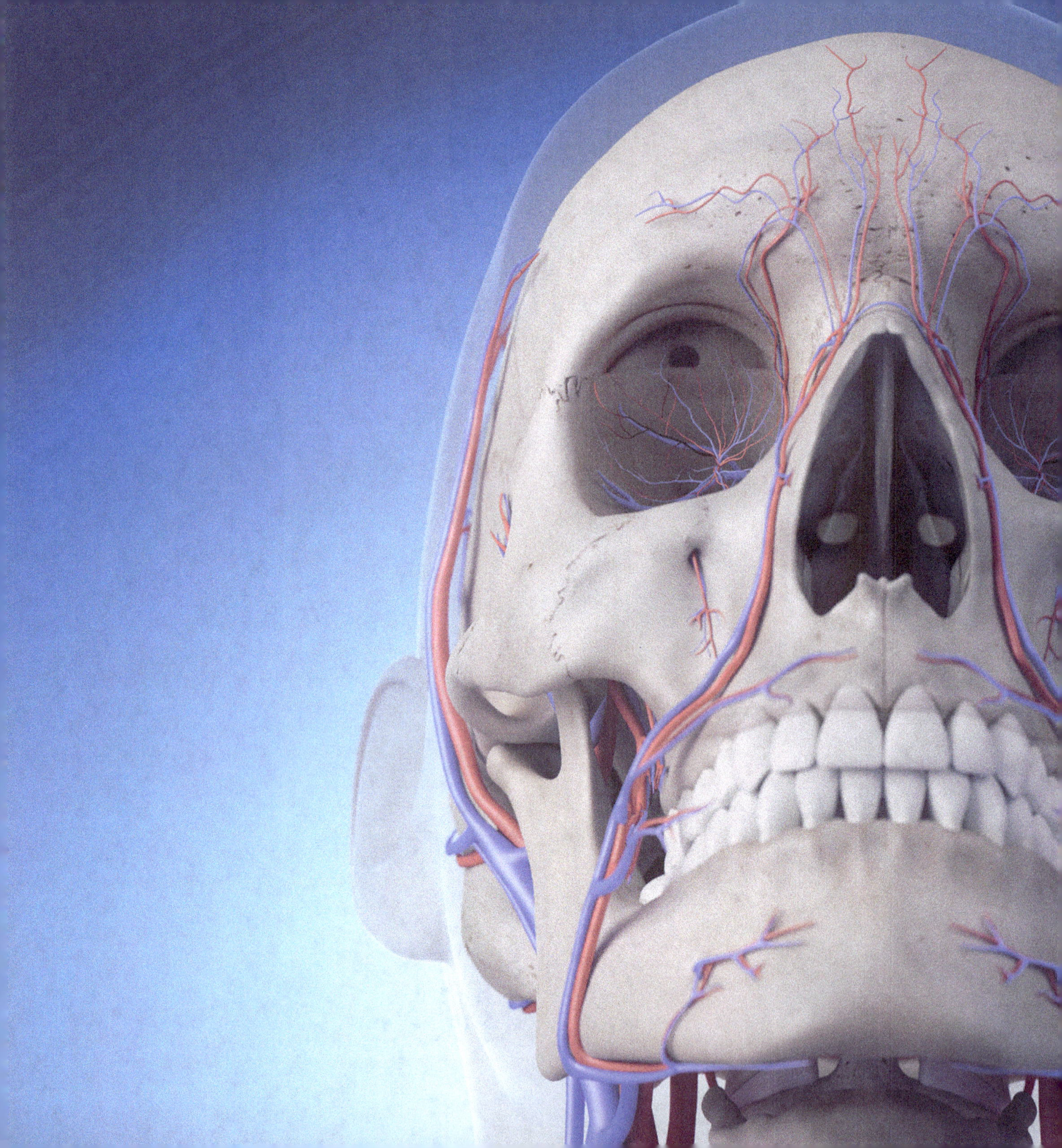

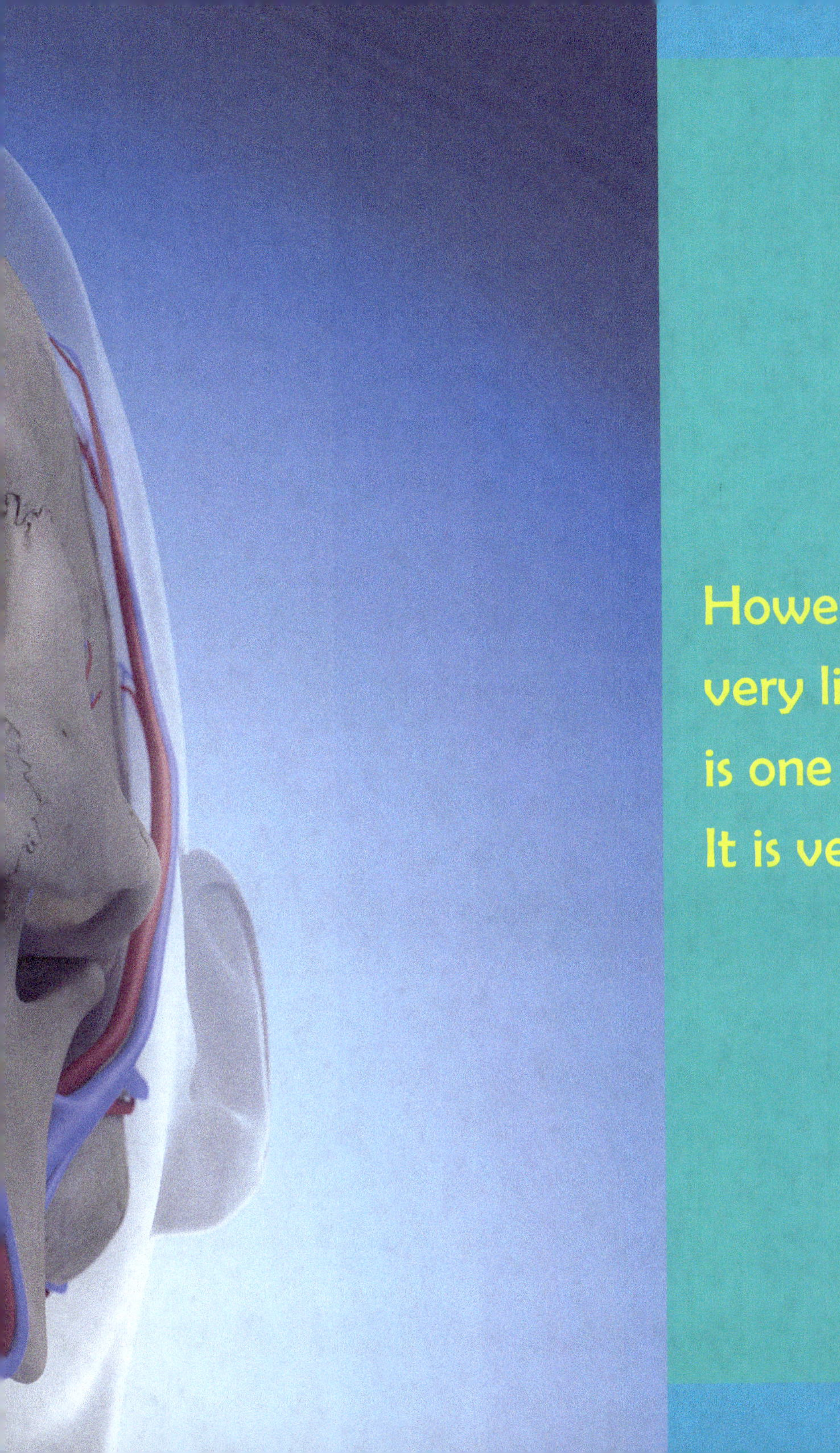

However, bones are very light. The skull is one of the bones. It is very strong.

It has the essential function of protecting our brain. The skull also protects our eyes, ears, and nose.

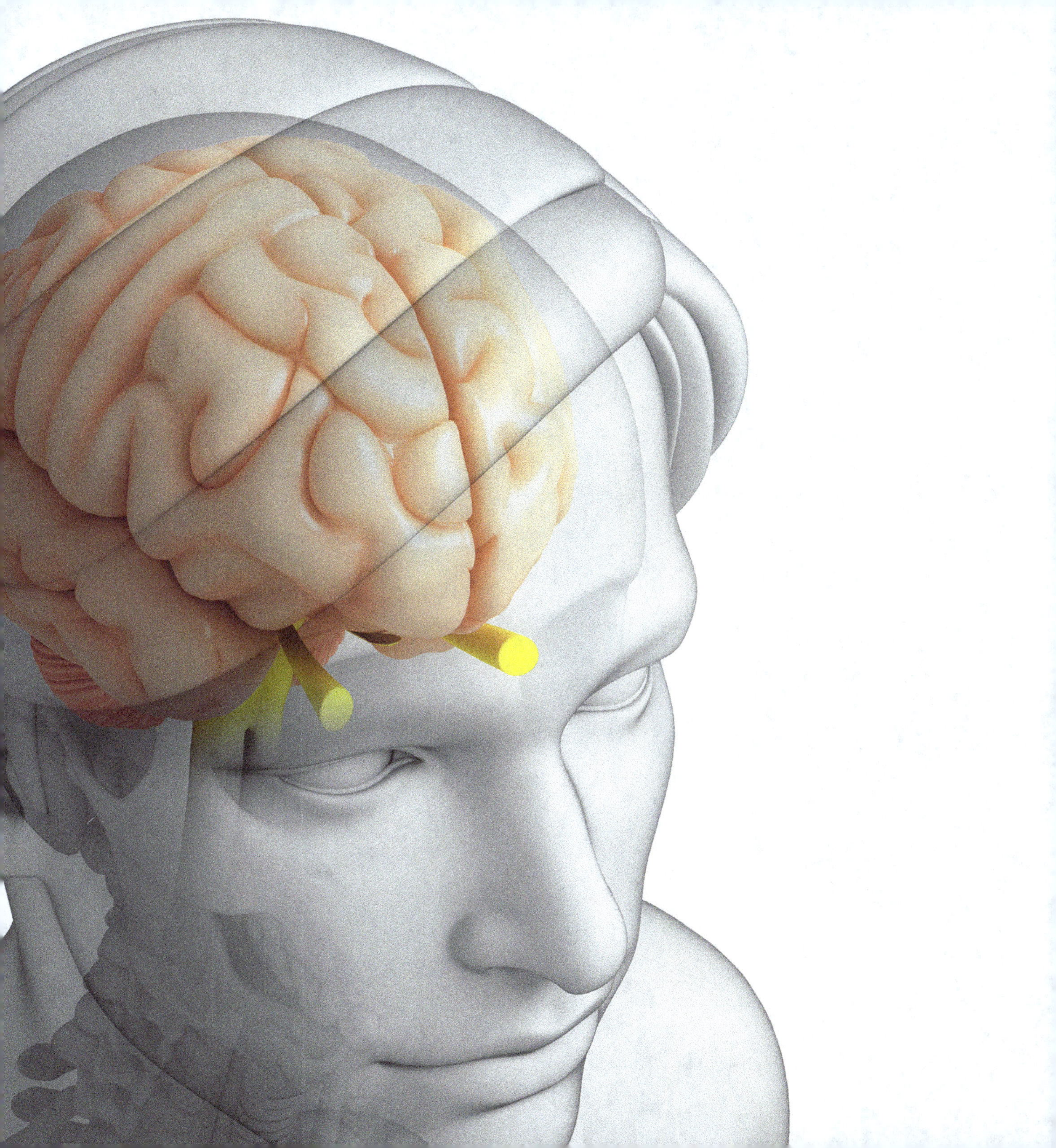

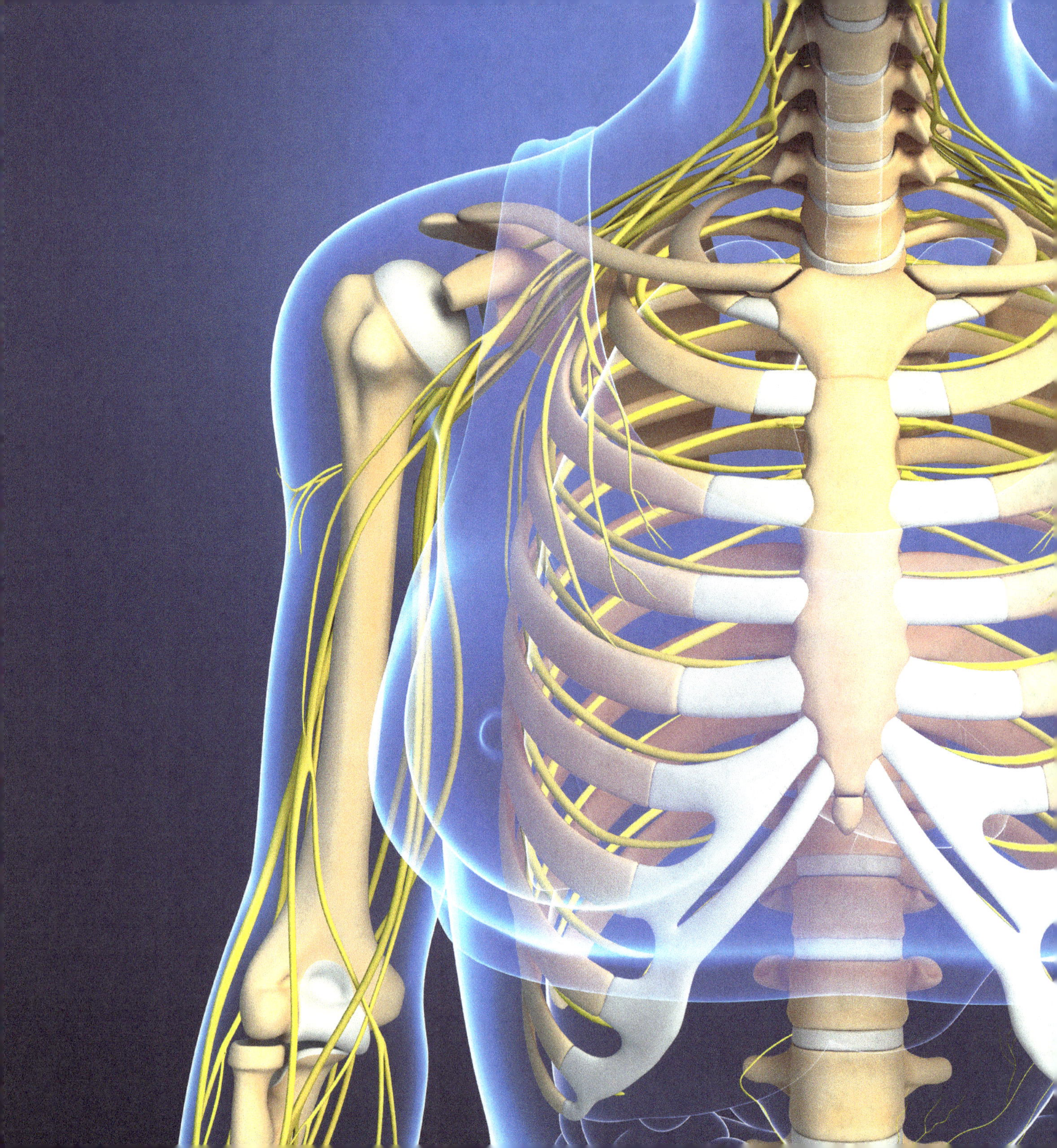

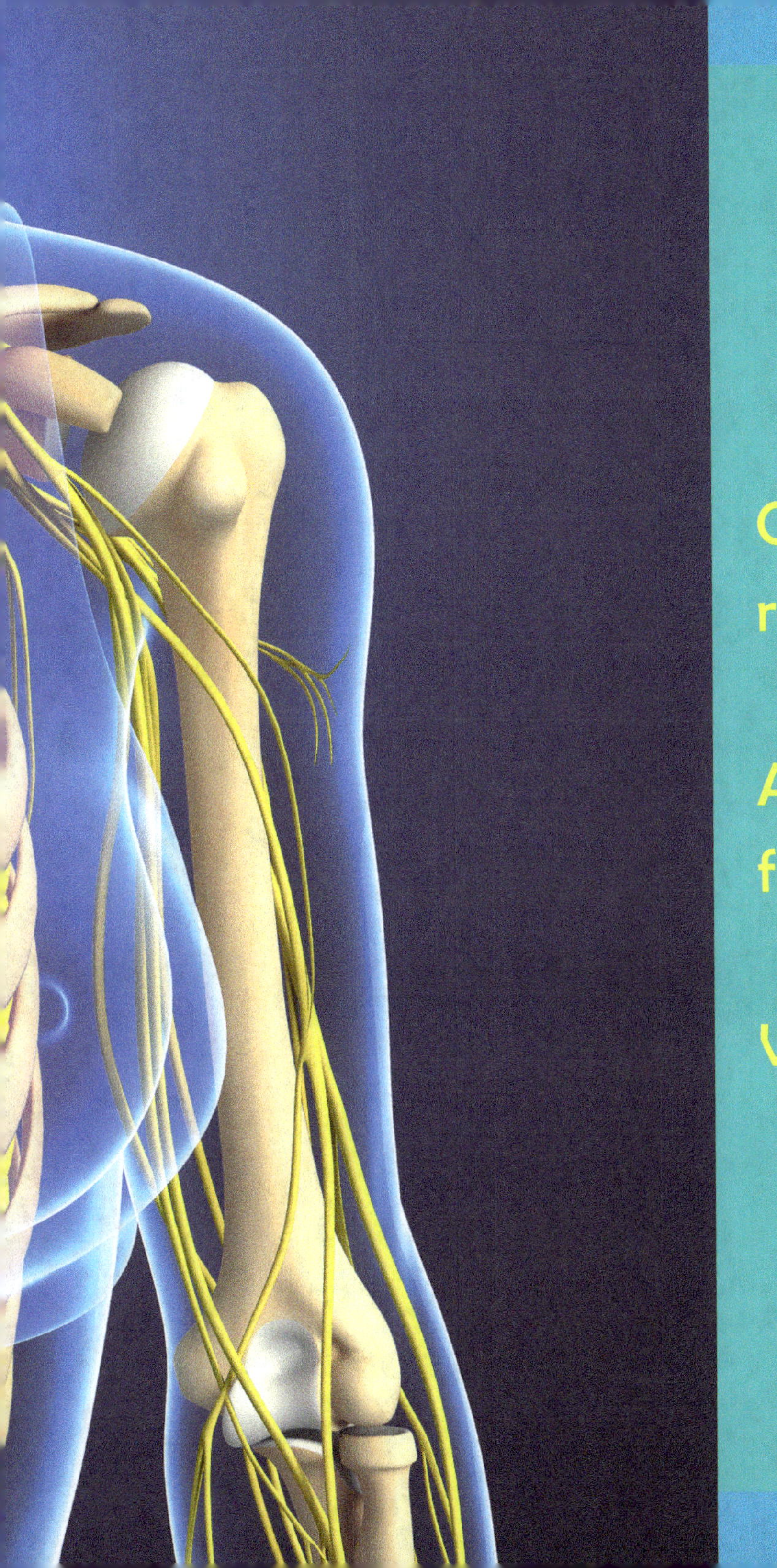

Our bones are
really amazing.

Are they really
flexible?

What do you think?

Our bones are
a little soft even
though they are
characterized as
very strong. Our
bones feel wet, too.

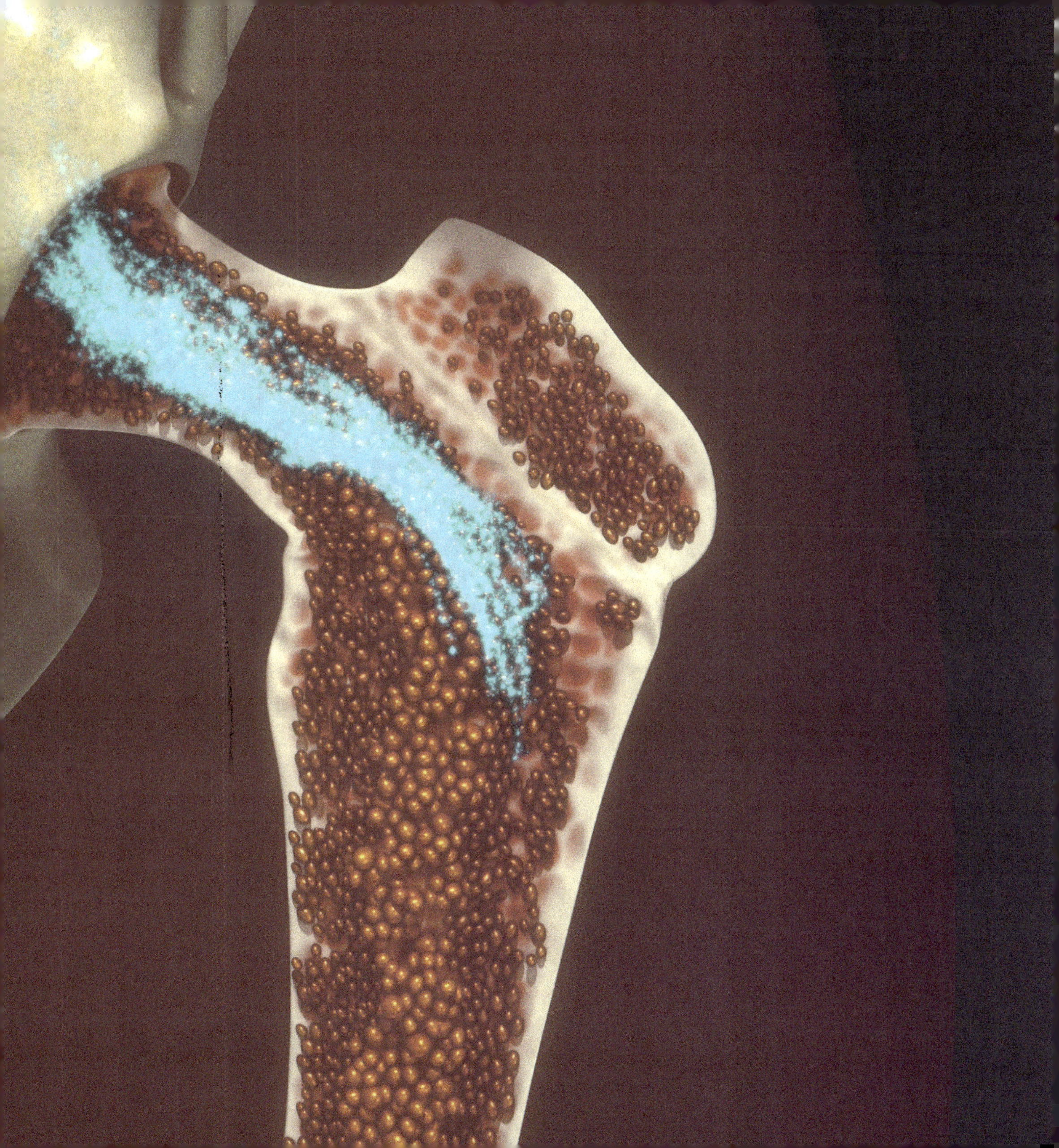

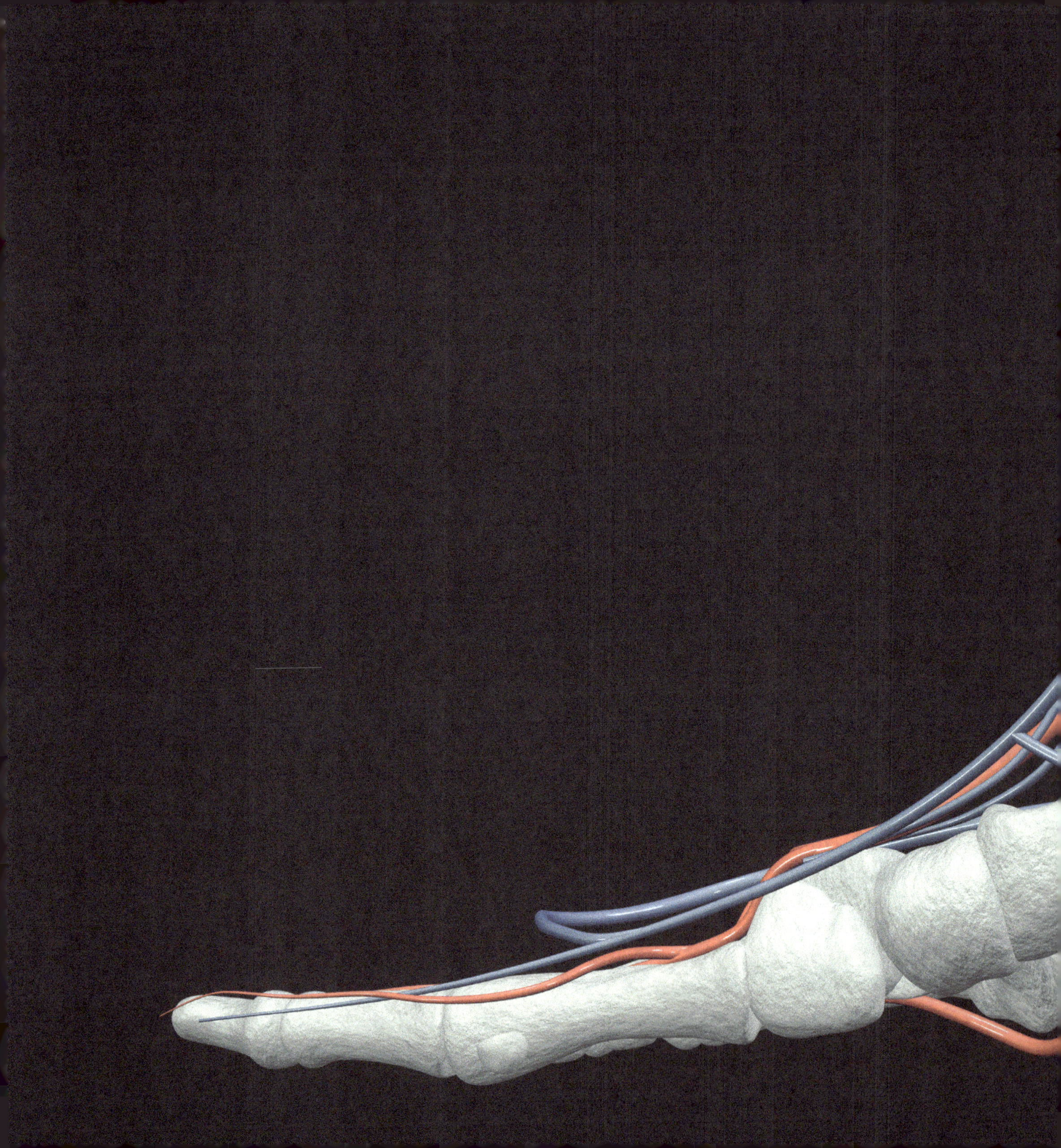

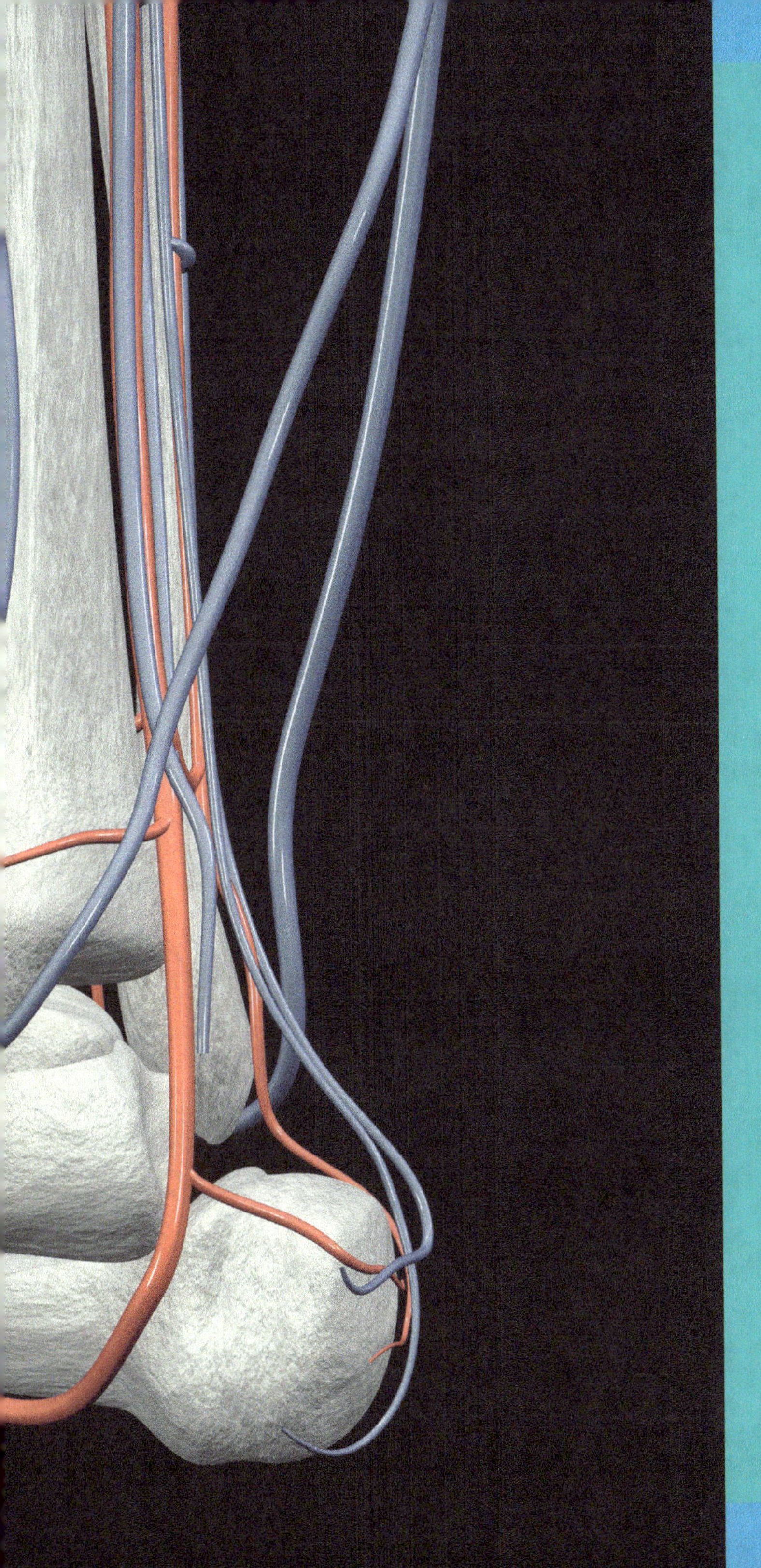

One-third of the weight of a living bone is water. Bones have blood vessels and nerves. They run through the bones.

That is why when
the bone breaks,
they bleed. Hence,
our bones are
really flexible.

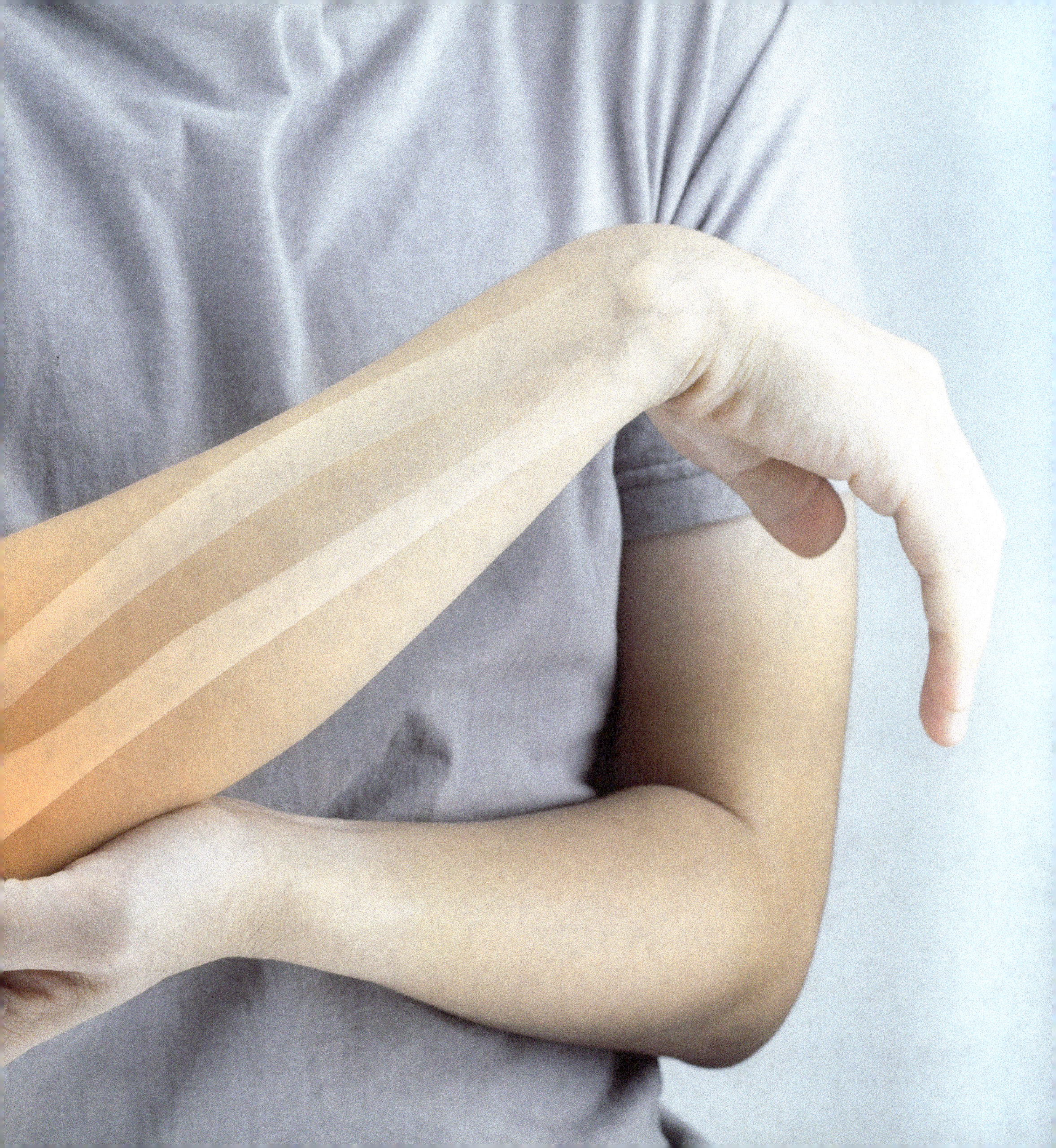

Amazingly, we can bend our bones. Absolutely, our bones are very strong yet flexible. Therefore, we come to know that our bones are not solid like pieces of rock.

They are living
tissues in the
body. Our bones
are made up of
bone cells. These
cells are joined
together by fibers.

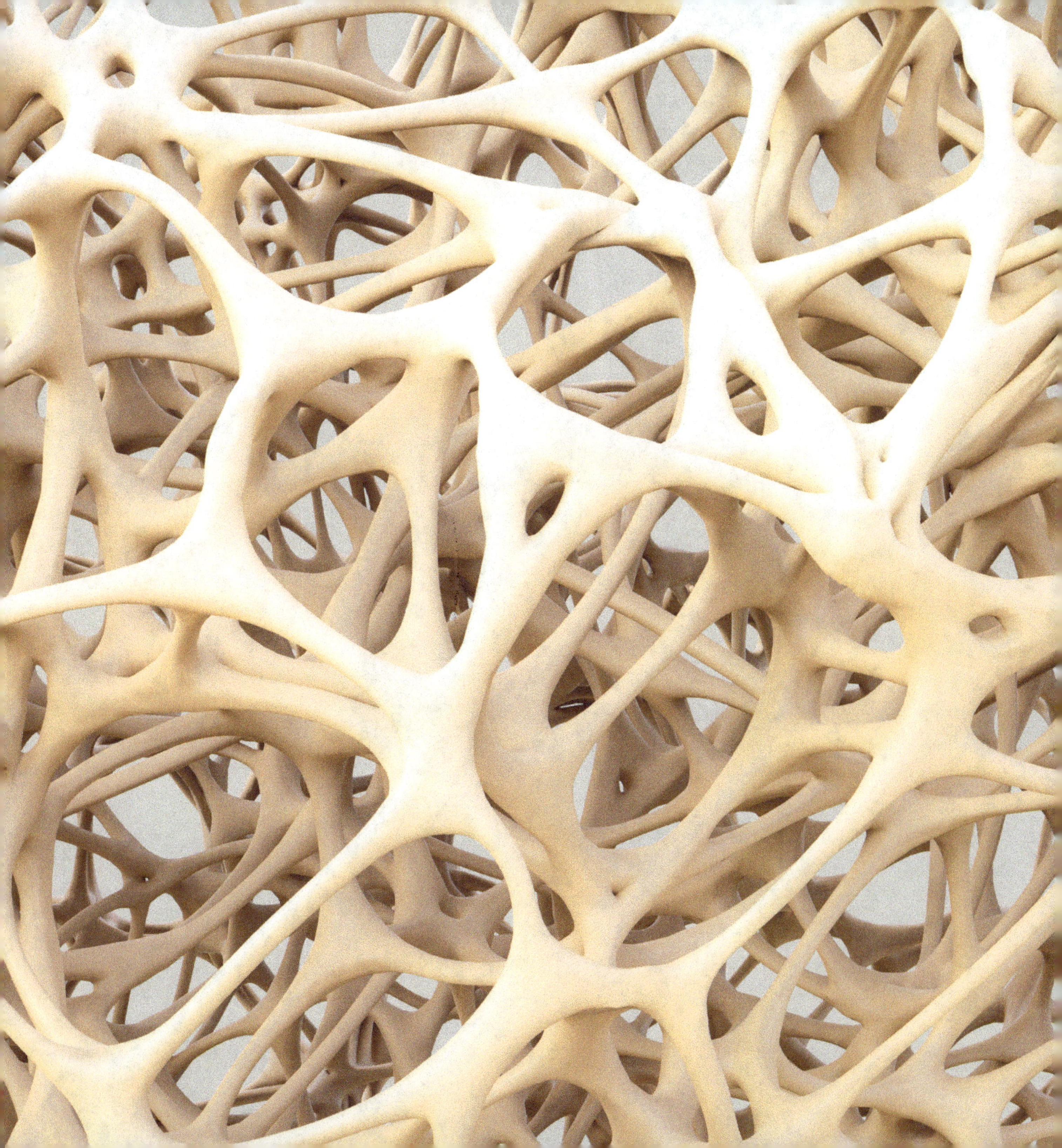

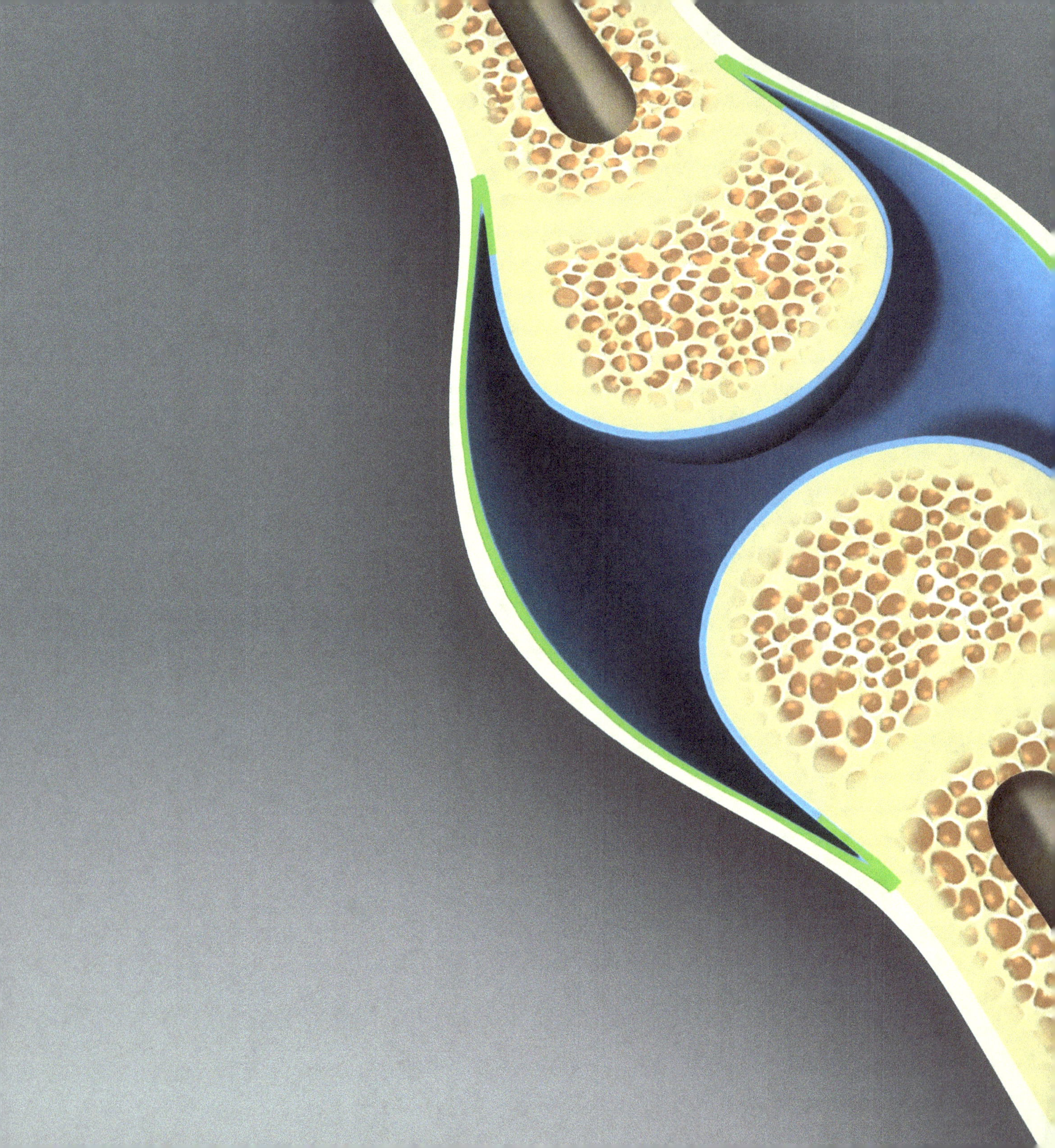

Our bones have
a strong outer
layer. Next to it is
the spongy part.
It has air in it
which makes the
bones so light.

**What do you
call that jellylike
substance at the
center of the bone?**

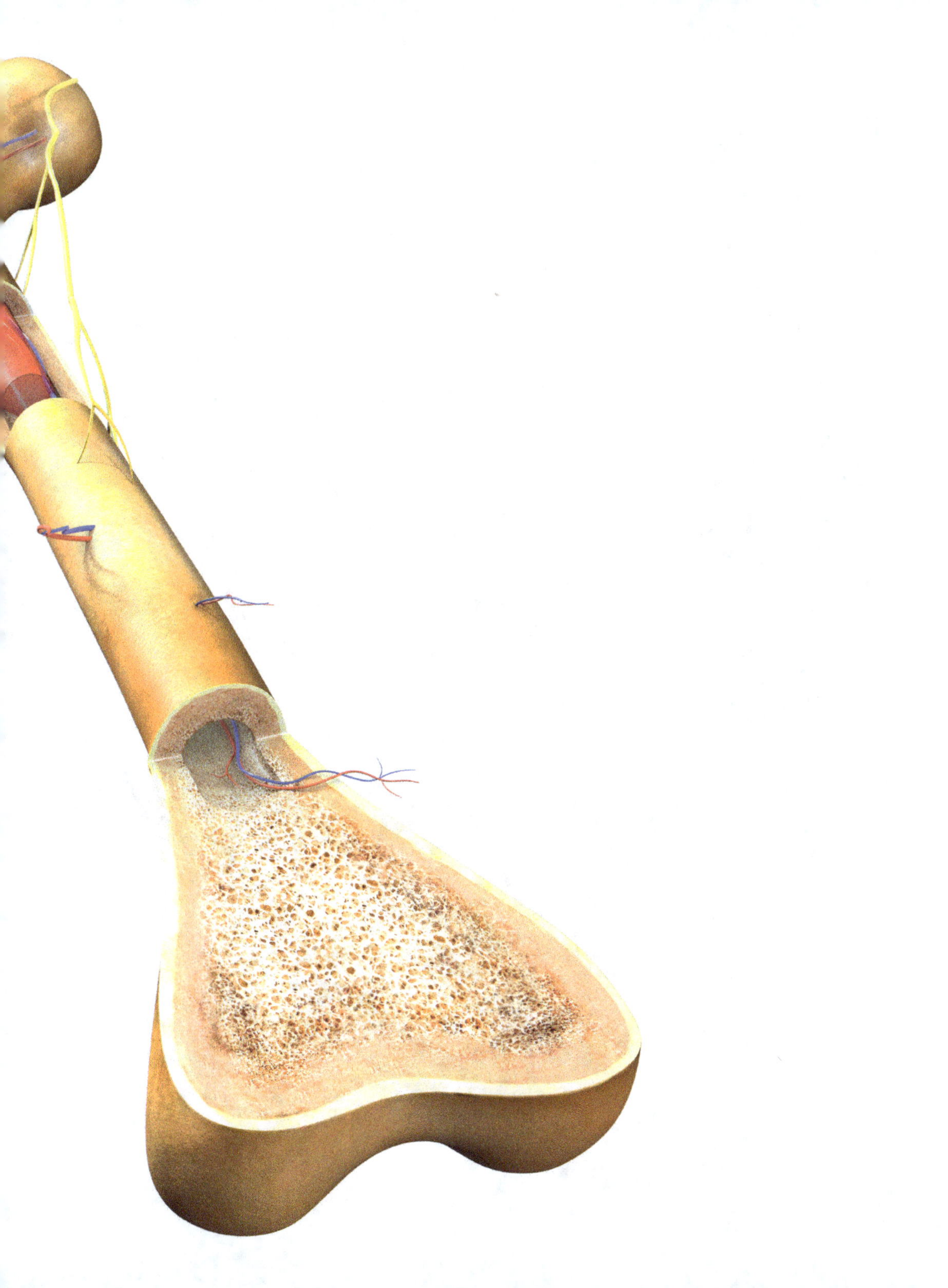

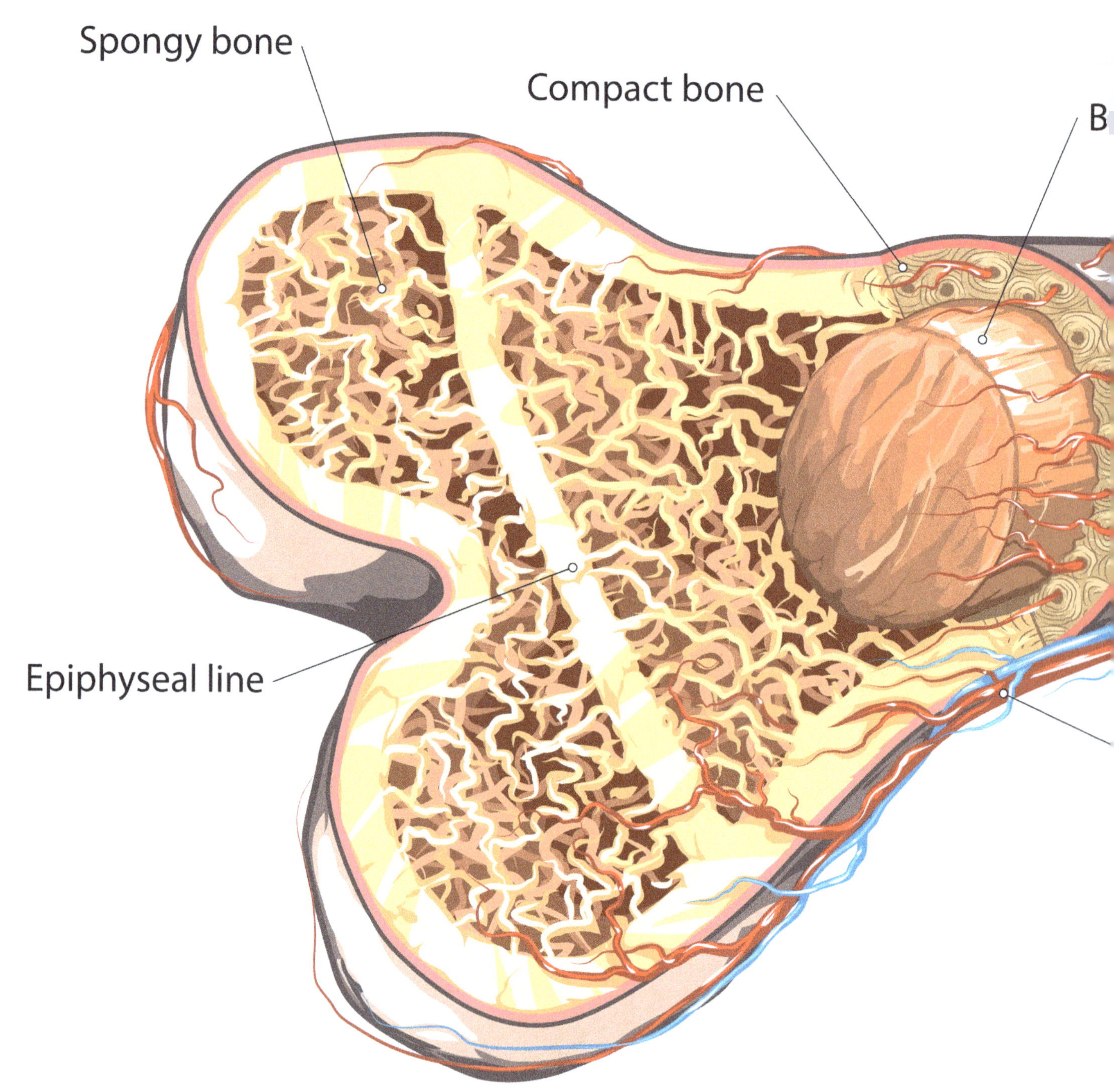

Spongy bone
Compact bone
B
Epiphyseal line

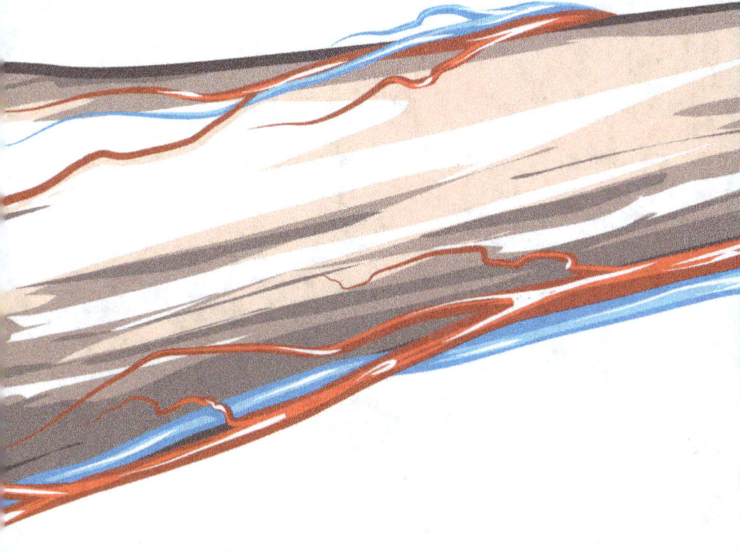

It is called bone marrow. It is a soft and flexible. The bone marrow does a very important function in the body. Millions of blood cells are made by the bone marrow.

The red blood cells
are responsible for
carrying oxygen
all throughout
the body. Our
bones work hard
to replace worn-
out cells with
fresh, new ones.

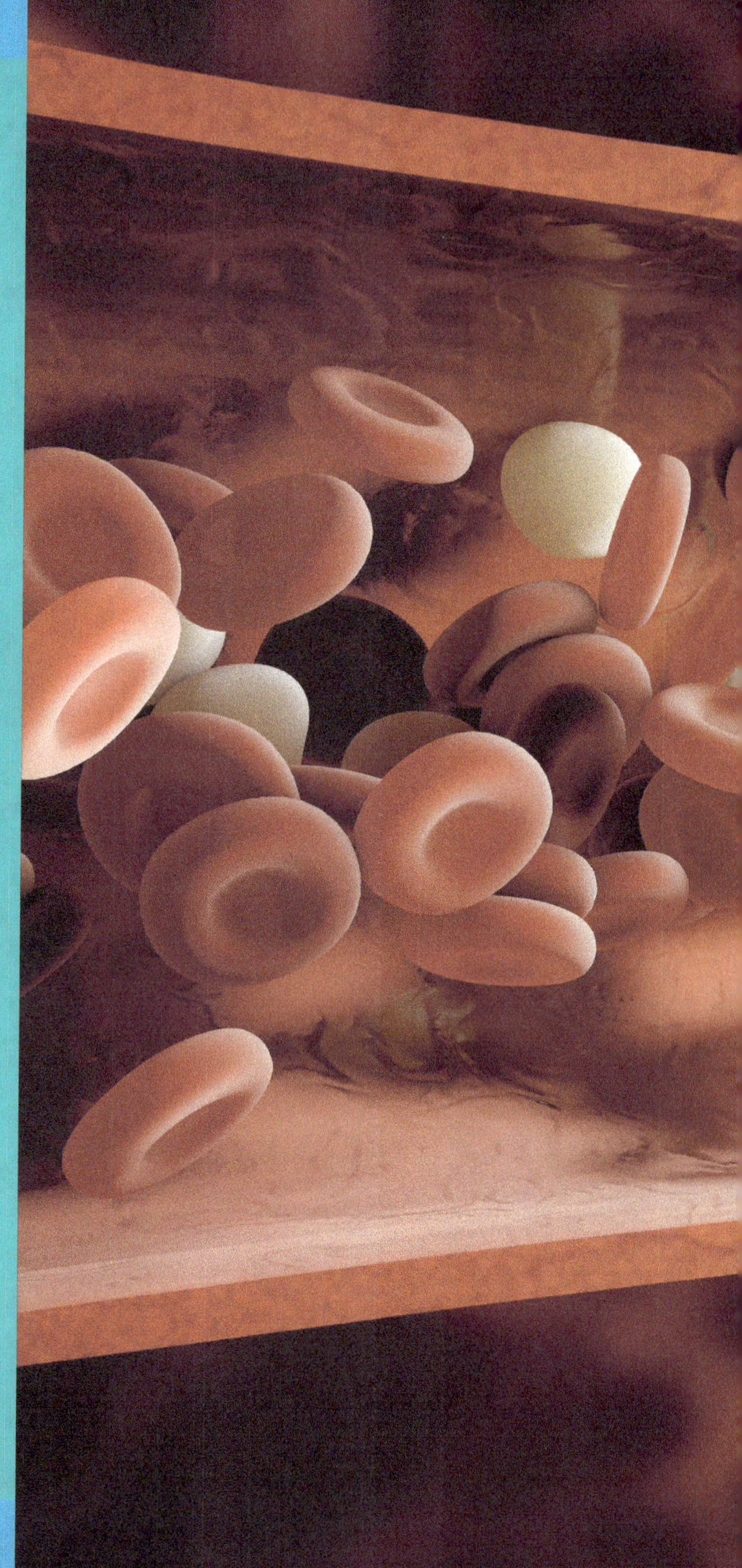

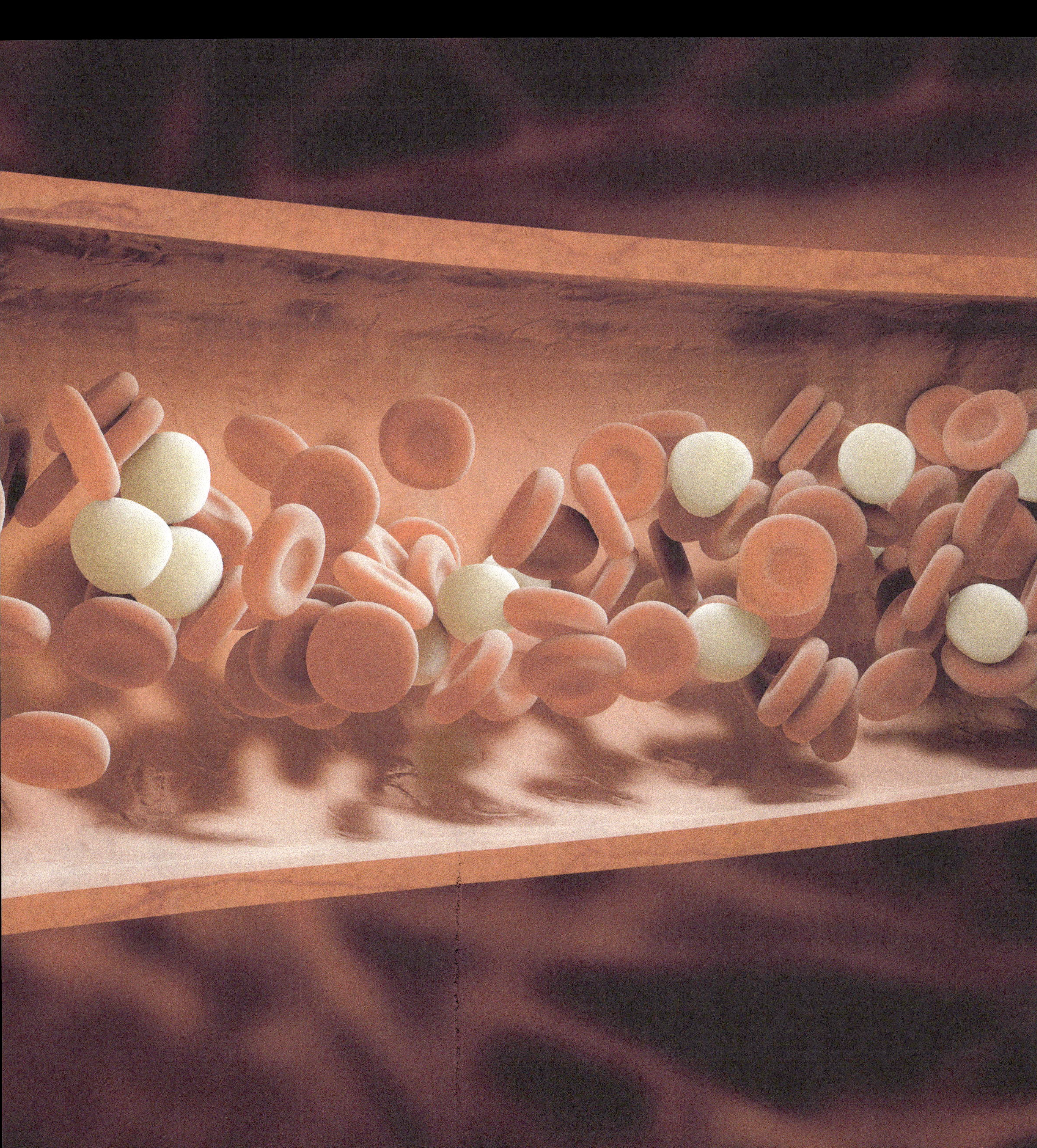

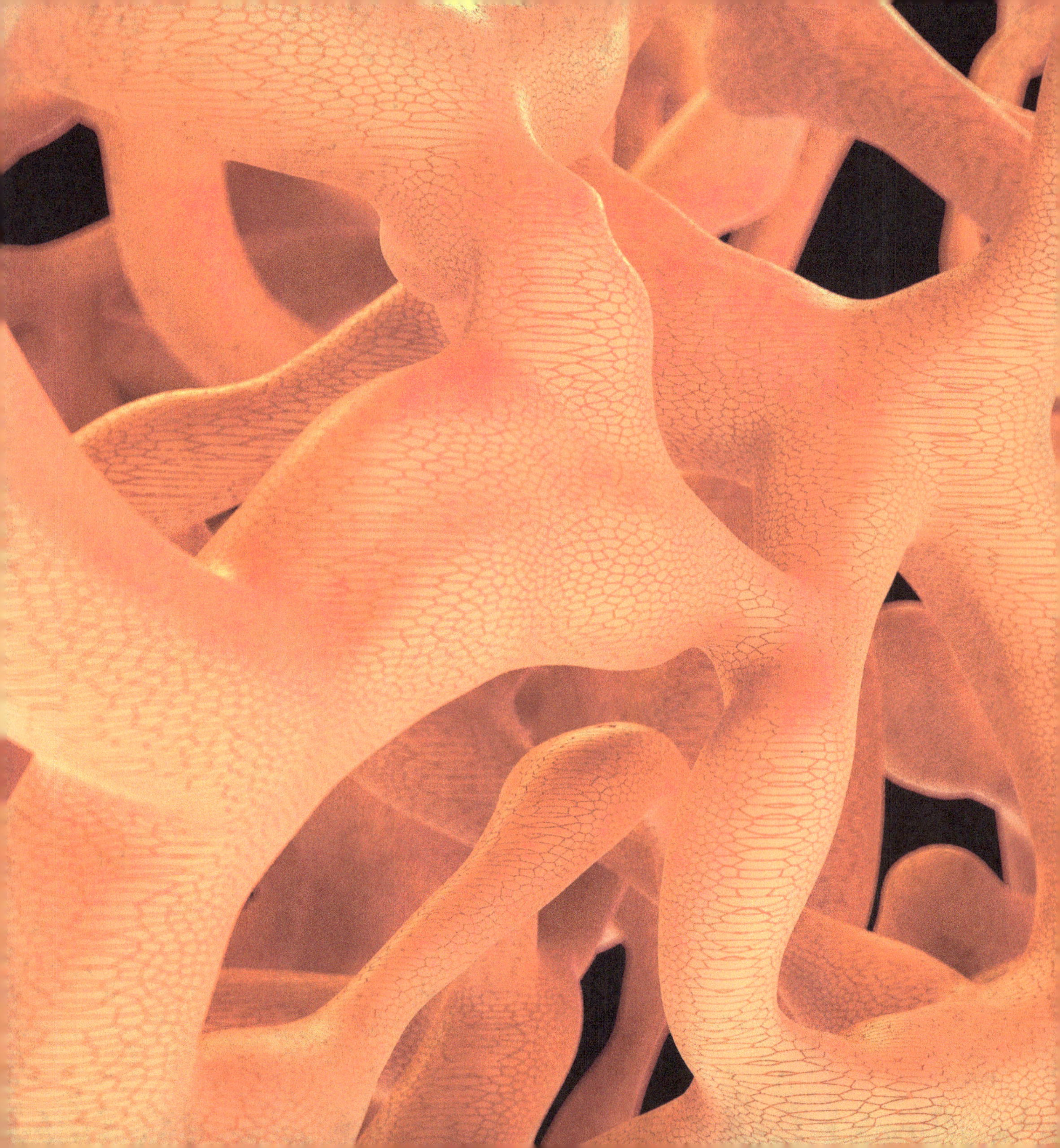

The two types of
bone marrow are
red marrow and
yellow marrow. It
is the red marrow
which makes
red blood cells.

What about the
yellow marrow?

It is there as a
reserve or as a fat
store. However,
if more blood
cells are needed,
yellow marrow
can amazingly
transform into
red marrow.

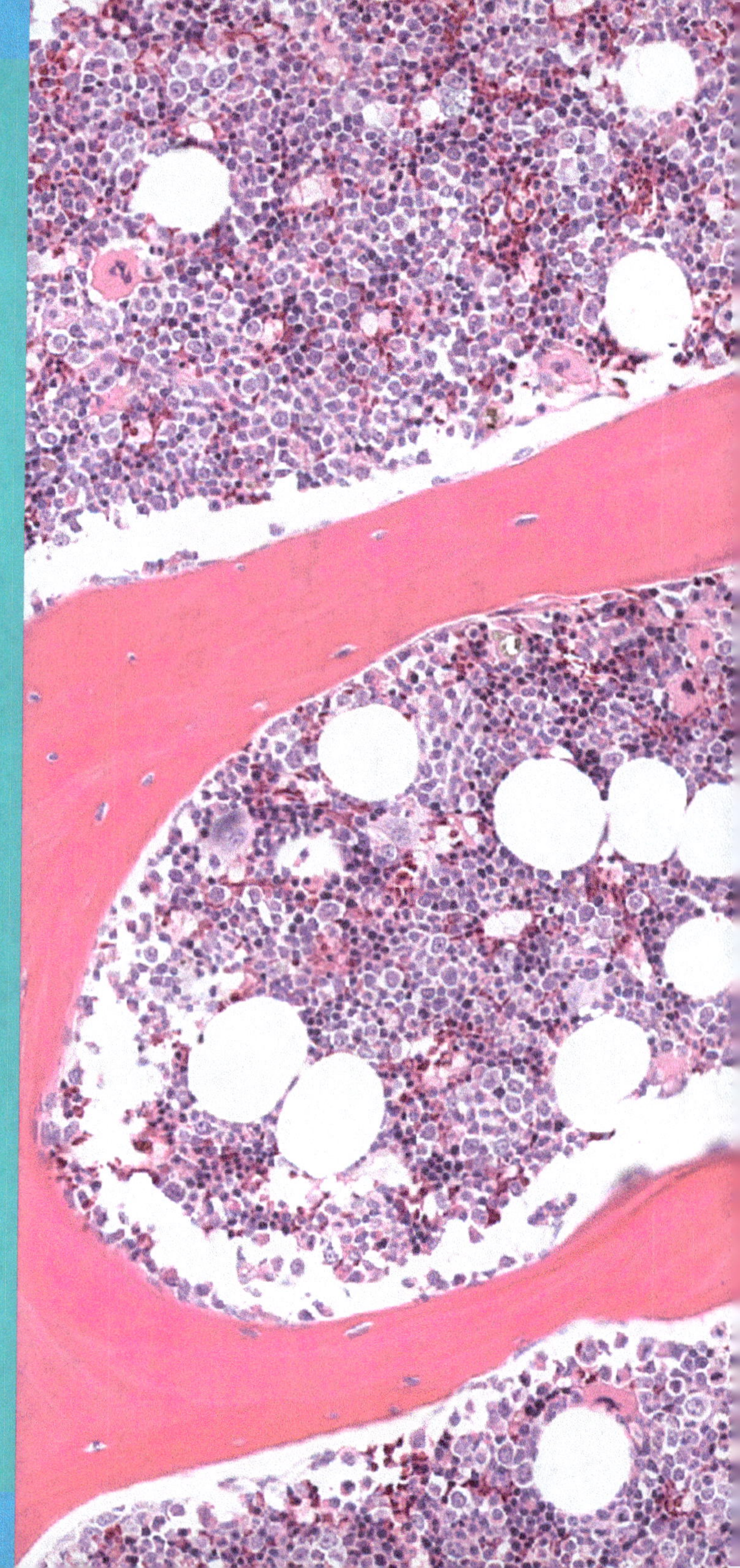

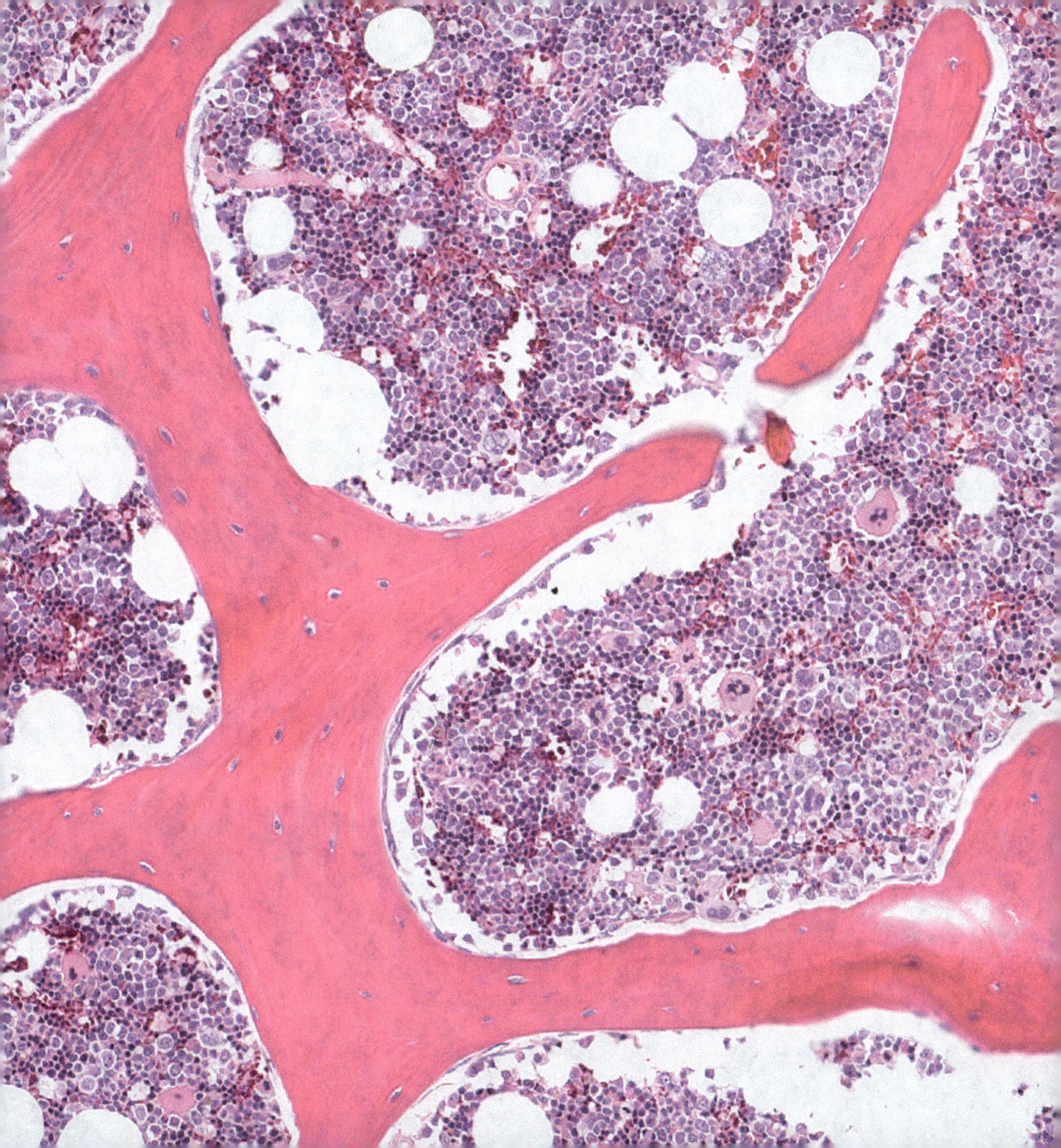

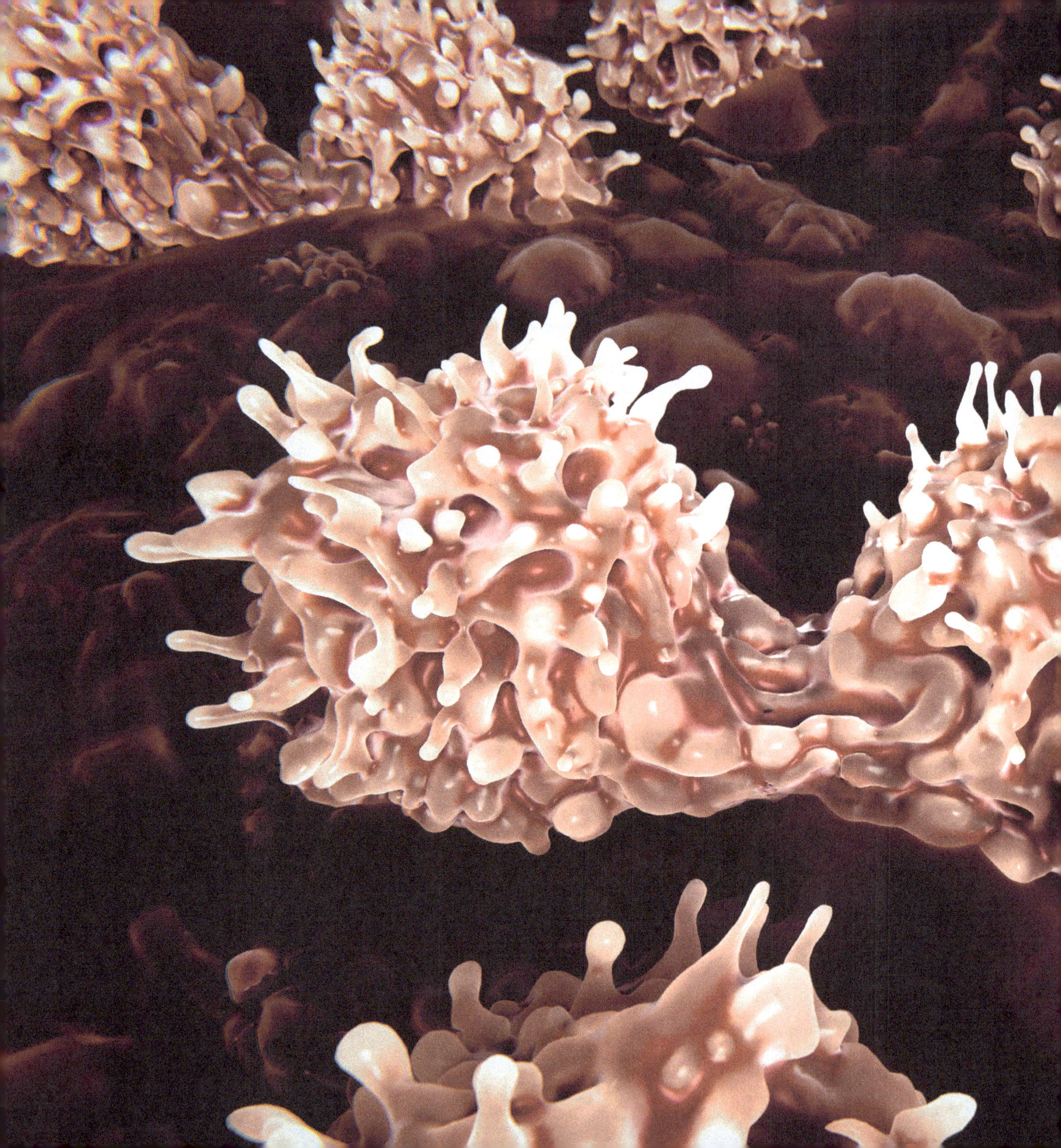

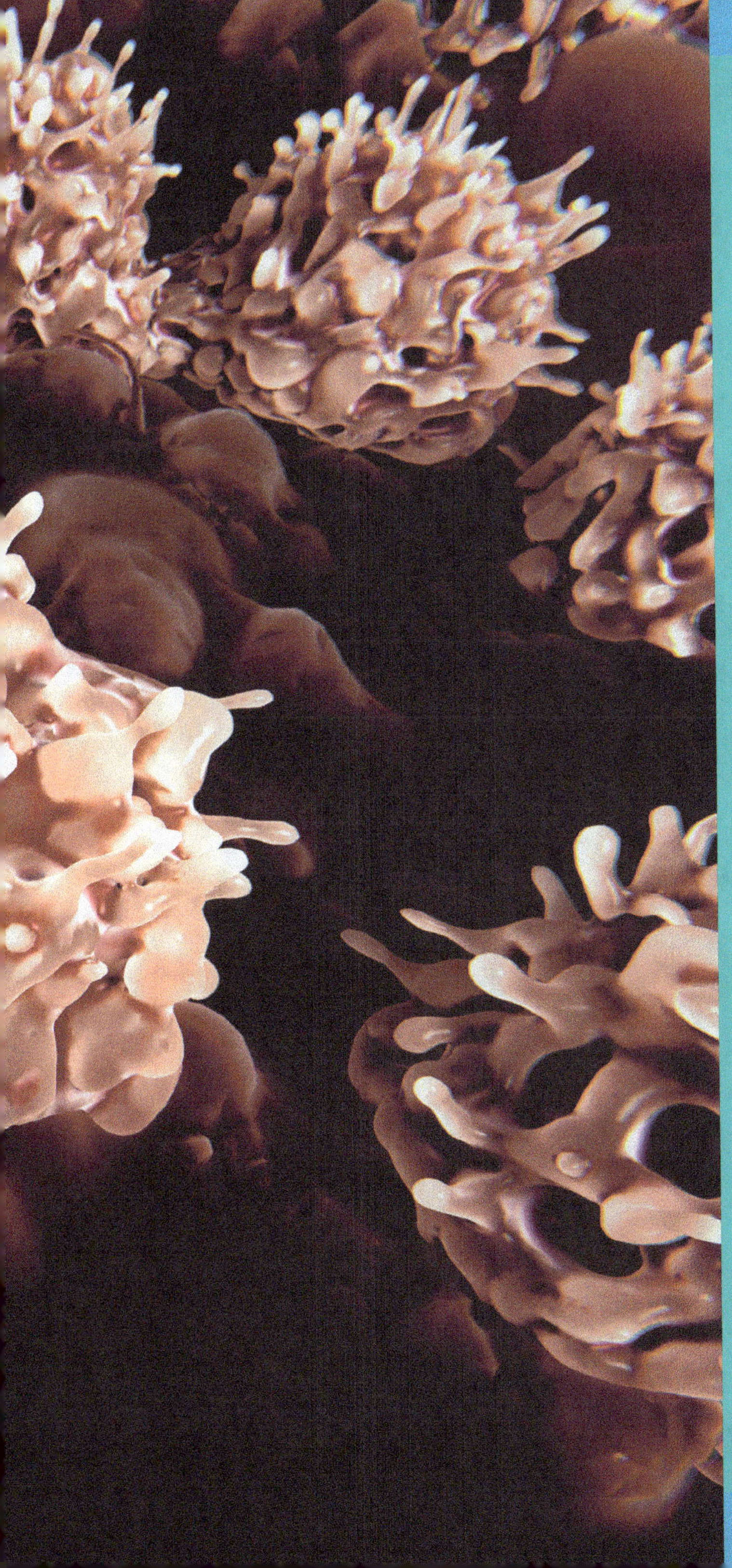

A baby's bone marrow is nearly all red. As the baby grows to a teenager, most of the red marrow turns to yellow bone marrow.

Our bones meet
at joints. Some of
these joints allow
body movements.
The bones are kept
together at joints
by fibrous tissues
known as ligaments.

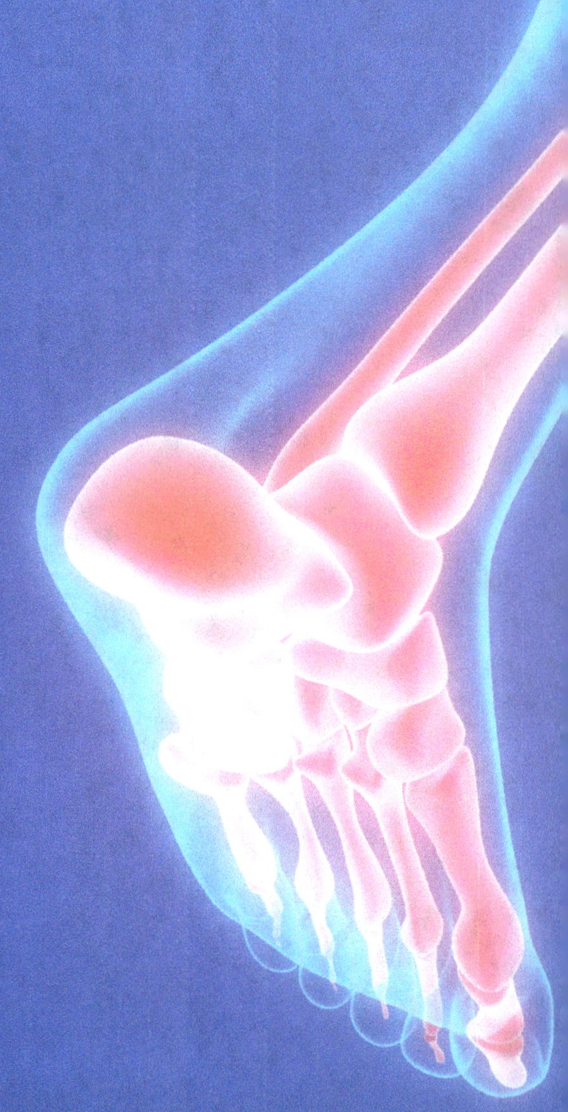

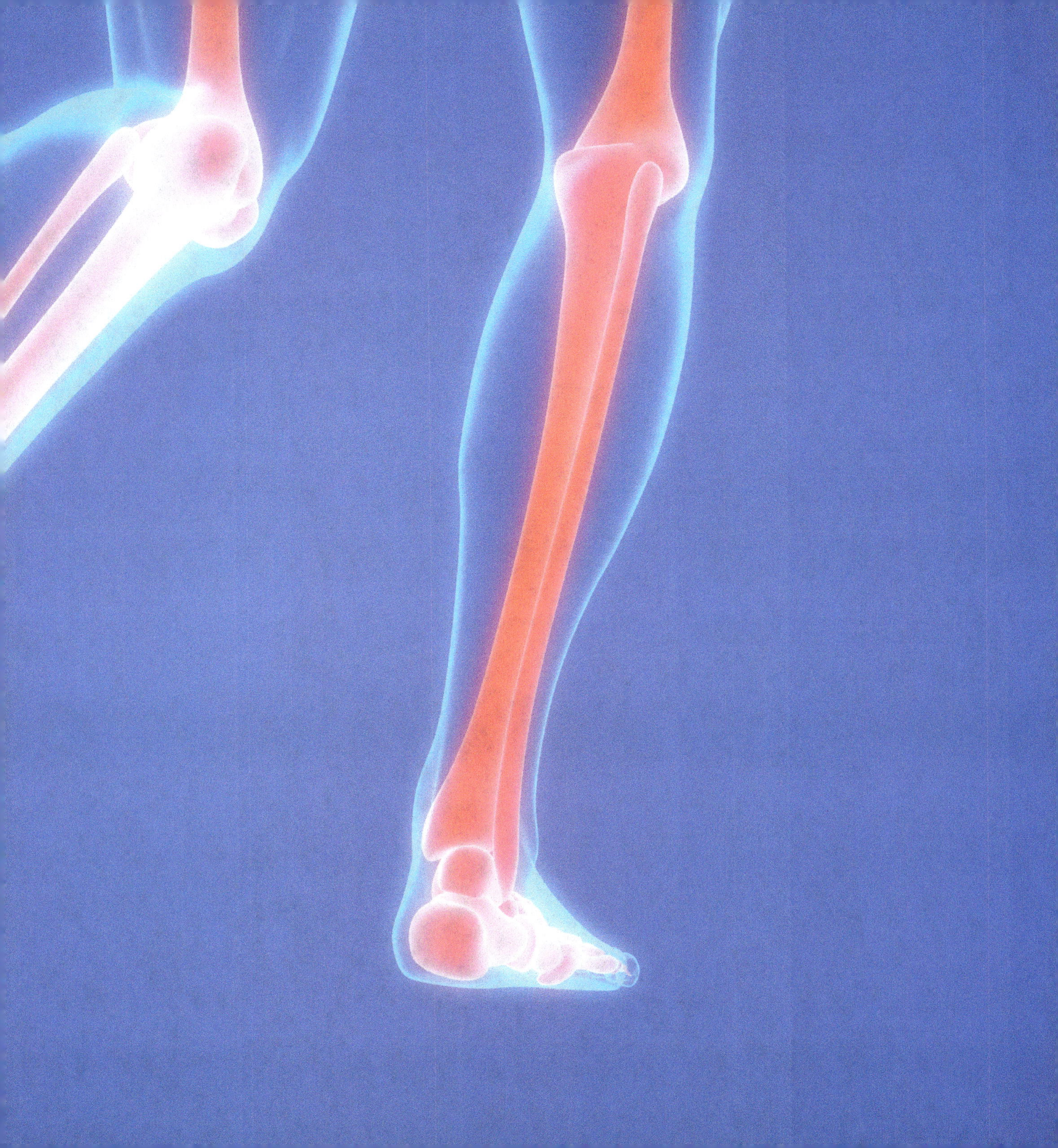

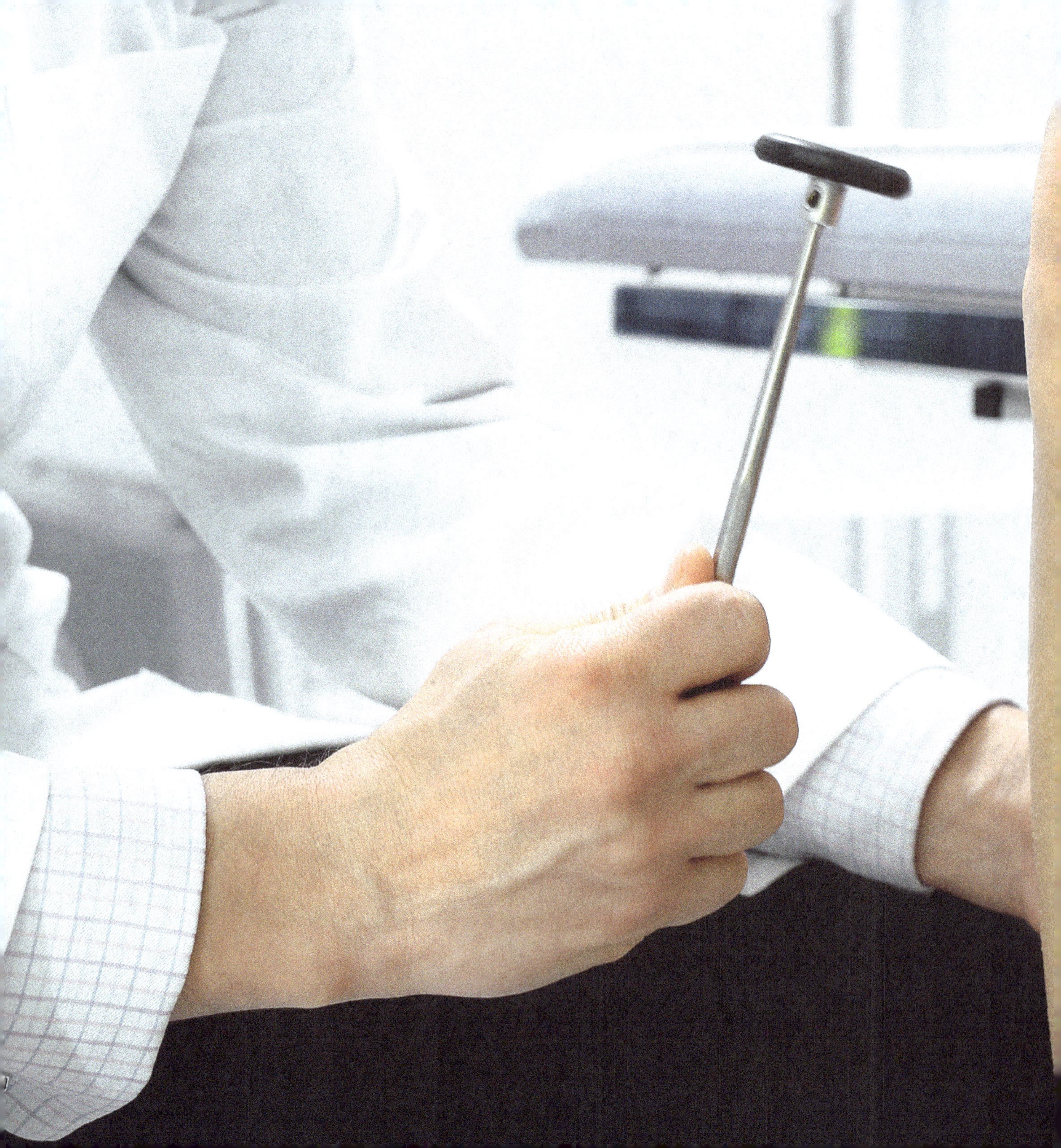

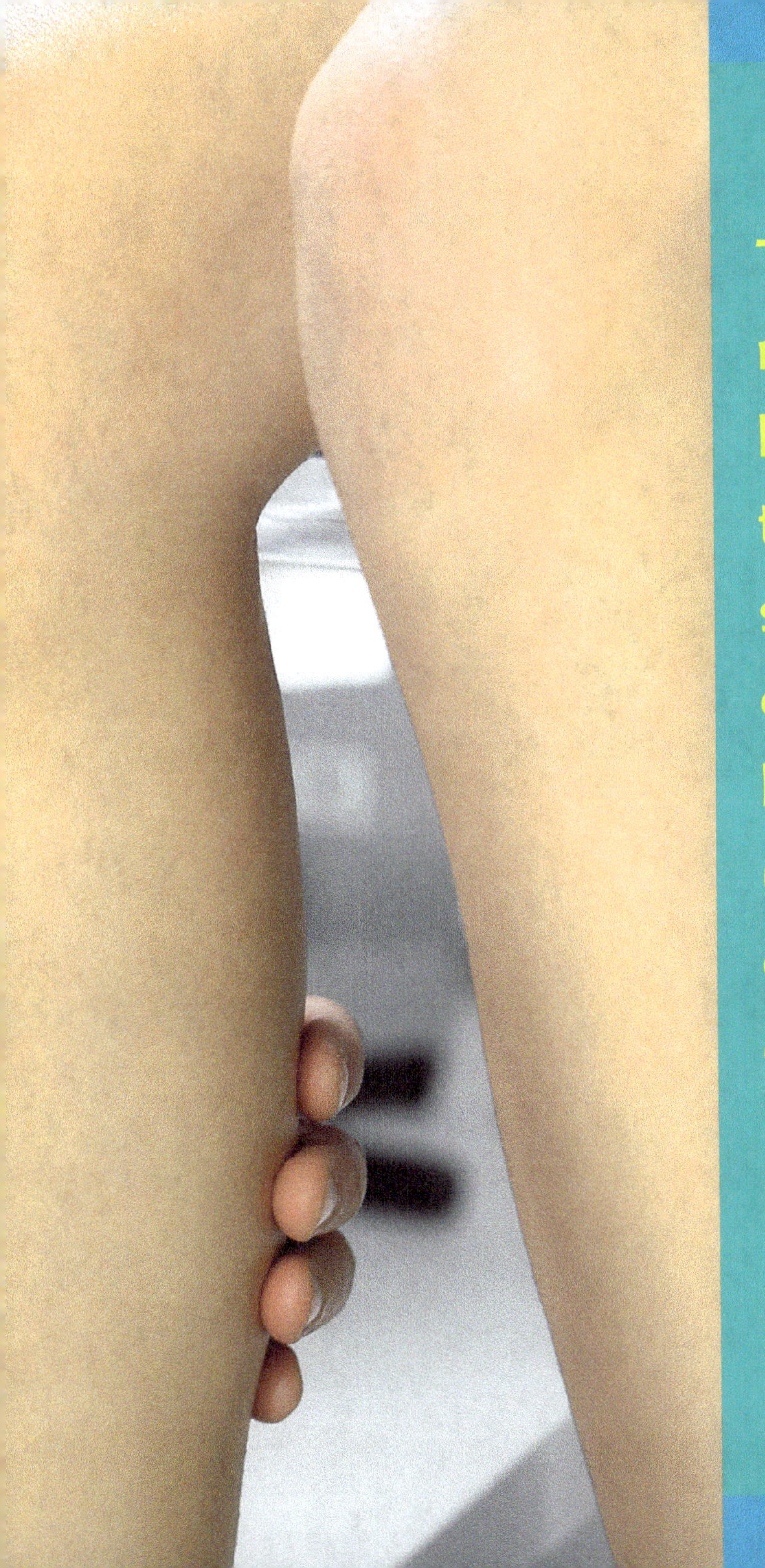

The branch of medicine which helps us learn about the human skeletal system is known as orthopedics. This branch helps people understand the different skeletal disorders which include scoliosis, osteoporosis, and arthritis.

Our bones are one of the amazing parts of the body. They perform amazing functions.

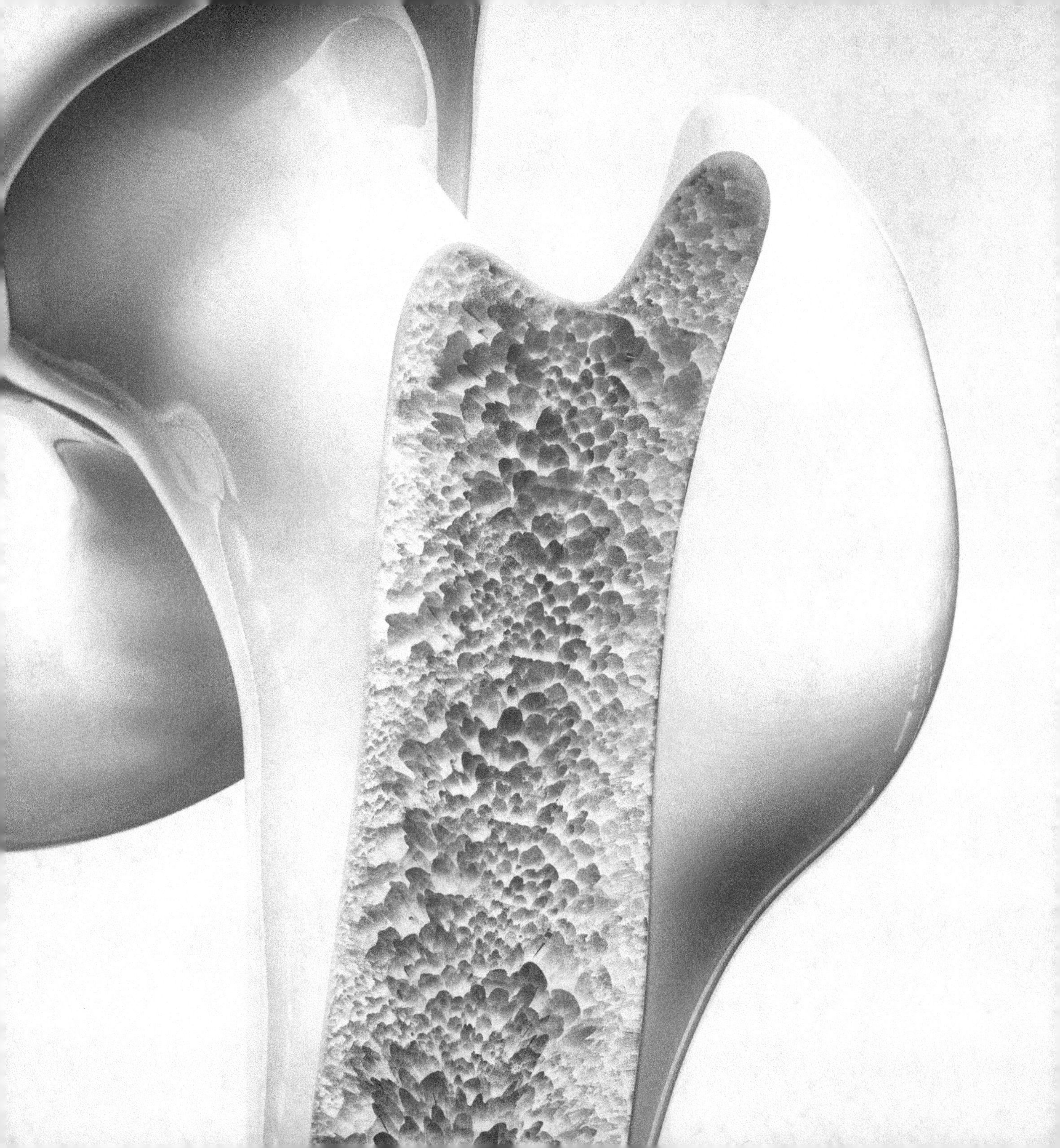

Hence, we should keep our bones strong and healthy.

Visit
BABY PROFESSOR
EDUCATION KIDS
www.BabyProfessorBooks.com
to download Free Baby Professor eBooks
and view our catalog of new and exciting
Children's Books